TRUTH, TRADITION, OR TARE?

Growing in the Word

A **BE KY** Book ©

Hollisa Alewine, PhD

DEDICATION

To all my teachers, past, present, and future.

CONTENTS

GLOSSARY

Adonai – my Lord.

Brit Chadasha – New Testament. In Hebrew, literally, "Renewed Covenant." The Hebrew word for new, *chadash*, also means renewed, as we apply the adjective to the New Moon. The moon is not new; it is the same moon. Its appearance is merely renewed each month. By the same token, Jeremiah 31:31 defines the terms of the New Covenant: the Torah will be written on the hearts of God's people. It is not a new Torah, but the old Torah renewed in a dynamic way because of the work of Yeshua, a better mediator than Moses.

Chiastic – A chiastic structure is a literary technique wherein a story is divided into two halves and the themes of the first half of the story are repeated in the second half of the story in reverse order. Furthermore, the two halves of the chiastic structure "point" to the most important element of the structure, the central axis. This is illustrated below:

A. Daniel 2: Four Gentile world empires
> B. Daniel 3: Gentile persecution of Israel
>> C. Daniel 4: Divine providence over Gentiles
>> C'. Daniel 5: Divine providence over Gentiles
> B'. Daniel 6: Gentile persecution of Israel
A'. Daniel 7: Four Gentile world empires

Elohim – God the Creator named in Genesis One

Erev Shabbat – the eve of Shabbat that starts at sundown on Friday evenings.

False dilemma – Oversimplification that offers a limited number of options (usually two) when in reality more options are available. A false dilemma arises when a trap is set to convince someone that there are two and only two mutually exclusive options, when that is untrue. Often one of the options is unacceptable and repulsive, while the other is the one the manipulator wants us to choose. Examples: "Are you a Republican or a Democrat?" "Do you support tax increases, or are you stingy?"

Halakha – Jewish law and jurisprudence, based on the Talmud. It describes how Israel will "walk" out the commandments, for the word is formed from the Hebrew verb *halakh*, walk.

Hermeneutics – Methods of Biblical interpretation applying accepted rules of interpretation.

Kal v'khomer – a principle that uses the relationship between "light" and "heavy" truths, so that if the "light" example is true, then how much more will the "heavy" example be true? For instance, Yeshua tells his disciples that if the Father cares for a sparrow that falls, then how much more will He care for a human being?

Logical fallacy –A logical fallacy is an error of reasoning. When someone adopts a position, or tries to persuade someone else to adopt a position, based on a bad piece of reasoning, it is a manipulation of thought.

Menorah – a lampstand, specifically, the seven-branched golden lampstand that stood in the Holy Place of the Tabernacle and Temple.

Metaphor – a thing regarded as representative or symbolic of something else, especially something abstract.

Minchag – an accepted tradition or group of traditions in Judaism observed by a community and unique to that community

Mishnah – the Jewish oral law traditionally believed to have been passed down from Moses. Yeshua usually upheld the oral law of the House of Hillel, but he overruled most of the oral laws of the House of Shammai. They were the two predominant schools of the Pharisees in the First Century.

Mitzvah – commandment

Moed(im) – alludes to seasons and the appointed feasts of Israel: Passover, Unleavened Bread, Firstfruits of the Barley, Firstfruits of the Wheat (Pentecost), Trumpets, Day of Atonement, and Tabernacles

Muktzah – something prohibited from being carried on Shabbat because it represents weekday work activities

Nefesh – the bundle of appetites, desires, emotion, and intellect.

Rebbe/Rabbi – a Jewish spiritual leader or teacher.

Ruach HaKodesh – Holy Spirit

Talmud – the largest body of Jewish law and commentary containing the Mishnah, Gemara, and Tosefta.

TANAKH – Old Testament. Tanakh is an acronym for Torah, Neviim, Ketuvim, or Law, Prophets, and Writings, the ancient divisions of the Hebrew Bible. The books of the Tanakh are the same as, but are not arranged in the same order as Christian Bibles.

Takkanah/takkanot – Directives enacted by Jewish scholars which have the force of law. The authority to enact takkanot is derived from Deuteronomy 17:11.

Torah – the first five books of the Bible, misunderstood as "law" in English translations. The Torah is more accurately God's teaching and instruction. It contains topics such as science, history, priestly procedures, civil statutes, ordinances, health, agriculture, commandments, prophecies, prayer, animal husbandry, architecture, civics, and many others. The root word of Torah comes from the Hebrew word *yarah*, which means "to hit the mark." Torah may also be used to refer to all of the Hebrew Bible, or even to its smallest meaning, a procedure. Torah may be used by Messianic Jews to refer to the entire Bible from Genesis to Revelation, for the Torah is the foundation for all the Scriptures. The Prophets point Israel back to the Torah. The Psalms teach one to love the Torah as King David loved it. The Writings teach the consequences of departing from the Torah and the rewards for returning to it. The New Testament brings the Torah to its fullest meaning in the person Yeshua the Messiah, and much of the New Testament quotes the Tanakh.

Tzedekah – often translated as "righteousness" or "justice" in English, tzedekah has a much broader meaning in both the Bible and Jewish tradition. It also includes the part of one's income that must be given to the poor. In Judaism, justice and righteousness cannot be disentangled from charity in meaning.

Yeshua – Jesus' Hebrew name; salvation.

PREFACE

TARE

A tare in Biblical times is thought to be the darnel, a weed that resembles a stalk of wheat or barley. When the **wheat** ripens, however, the stalk head of grain will bow, while **the tare does not**, holding its heads of grain straight and high. At harvest time the tares can be separated without uprooting the wheat alongside which the tare grows.

WHEAT

Wheat was first cultivated in the ancient Near East, and it is **a vital indicator of a nation's well-being**. Its importance is emphasized when the judgment of famine is described as breaking the "staff of bread": "...the deadly arrows of famine which were for the destruction of those whom I will send to destroy you, then I will also intensify the famine upon you and break the staff of bread.[1]" The symbol of the staff with vital bread implies **authority, continuity, and control**. Wheat and barley were critical to the ancient economy; therefore, the wheat crop was the foodstuff of national survival, and its failure was considered Divine judgment.

INTRODUCTION

Readers of the Newer Testament can find its treatment of tradition confusing. Many of the customs in its pages are Jewish, and therefore foreign to non-Jewish believers. Yeshua (Jesus) sometimes corrected those observing religious customs, yet at other times he said they *should* have observed them. Paul does the same in his letters, and twice he instructs non-Jewish believers to keep the Jewish customs he passed on to them.

Among believers in Yeshua today, some enjoy incorporating tradition into their worship. Some dismiss all customs as "man-made," and therefore extraneous at best or the sin of "adding to" the written Word at worst. There is a way to determine the relationship of the written Word to tradition, for the Word would not leave us without comfort on such an important question. Our Father wants His children to grow in wisdom, maturity, and favor before Him as well as their communities.

The methods used by the prophets of the Older Testament (TANAKH) as well as the writers of the Newer Testament (*Brit HaChadasha*) did leave readers guidelines to divide the Seed of truth from tradition, and then to separate a tradition grown from truth from a "taredition" grown from a different seed. Additionally, it is just as important to the disciple of Yeshua to test the goodness of the soil on which the practice of the Word grows.

The most important consideration in the Older Testament's, Yeshua's, and the apostles' instructions is the sincere heart that holds justice, mercy, and faithfulness as the weightier matters of any religious custom. By evaluating the traditions that one chooses to observe or not observe, the individual

1. Ezek 5:16

13

can avoid the lament:

> O Lord, my strength and my
> stronghold, my refuge in the day
> of trouble, to you shall the nations
> come from the ends of the earth
> and say: 'Our fathers have inherited
> nothing but lies, worthless things in
> which there is no profit.' [2]

By applying the instructions in the Word, every believer is encouraged in his or her growth. The tests of how one practices a personal walk in the Word are distilled into simple steps:

> 1. Is it the Seed of Truth? His Word is Truth. [3]
> 2. Is it tradition? From what seed did the tradition grow?
> 3. Who is glorified through the tradition? What is the condition of the soil from which the tradition grows?

A careful examination of Yeshua's instructions lifts a nuance that is frequently lost in discussions of truth and tradition. The first step is to identify whether that tradition is a tare. By throwing all tradition into a mental trash bin labeled Man's Tradition, it is possible that one could throw good plants and fruit into the bin with the tares. This is a logical fallacy called oversimplification. Yeshua's parables encourage his disciples to learn critical thinking skills so that growth in the Word is abundant life.

When a disciple of Yeshua examines his or her walk in the Word, there may be times that he or she feels that there is not enough growth. The very fact that we question our growth is a sign of readiness to grow. The next step is to allow the Holy Spirit (*Ruach HaKodesh*) to teach us how to bear good fruit. To do that, every disciple can identify beliefs and

2. Je 16:19 ESV

3. John 17:17

14

practices that either stimulate healthy growth in the Word, or they stunt it. Welcome to the living fields of the Father's Garden!

1

TRADITION OR TAREDITION

The seven-branched menorah (lamp) figures prominently in Scripture. According to the Book of Revelation, this lamp represents the Seven Spirits of God[4] as well as the seven sacred assemblies, or *moedim*[5], that correspond to each spirit (see Appendix A). The foundation is the seven days of Creation, the seven days on which the gospel was spoken, written, and counted into the realms of heaven and earth. In Revelation, Yeshua (Jesus) provides context for the reader; he refers to himself as the "Alpha and Omega, the Beginning and the End."

The hint to the reader is that Yeshua's message spans from the first verse of Genesis "In the beginning..." to the last verse of Revelation, "The grace of the Lord Jesus be with all. Amen." Teaching from the beginning to the present as well as prophetic future was Yeshua's pattern of teaching both his own disciples and the religious challengers. He started at the beginning with the Law (Torah)[6] and worked his way forward. As an example:

- Then beginning with Moses and with all the prophets, He explained to them the things

4. "And the spirit of the LORD shall rest upon him, the spirit of wisdom and understanding, the spirit of counsel and might, the spirit of knowledge and of the fear of the LORD;" (Isaiah 11:2 KJV)

5. The moedim are the feasts listed in the Torah: Passover, Unleavened Bread, Firstfruits of the Barley, Feast of Weeks, Feast of Trumpets, Day of Atonement, and Tabernacles. See *Creation Gospel Workbook One* by the author for a complete explanation of the parallels between the Seven Churches of Revelation and the Seven Feasts.

6. For a full explanation of the Torah, see BEKY Book *What is the Torah?* by the author.

17

concerning Himself in all the Scriptures.[7]
- And He said to him, 'What is written in the Law? How does it read to you?'[8]
- Now He said to them, 'These are My words which I spoke to you while I was still with you, that all things which are written about Me in the Law of Moses and the Prophets and the Psalms must be fulfilled.'[9]
- And He answered and said to them, 'What did Moses command you?'[10]

Yeshua was resolute in engaging doctrinal discussions at the foundational level. This level is called "Moses" or "Law" in English Newer Testament translations, and in Judaism, it is the "Torah." The beginning of the Scriptures describes the shadows of Messiah, yet throughout history, mankind has notoriously missed the mark of those Scripture shadows.

> You search the Scriptures because you think that in them you have eternal life; it is these that testify about Me; and you are unwilling to come to Me so that you may have life.[11]

7. Lk 24:27

8. Lk 10:26

9. Lk 24:44

10. Mk 10:3

11. John 5:39–40

12. A logical fallacy is an error of reasoning. When someone adopts a position, or tries to persuade someone else to adopt a position, based on a bad piece of reasoning, it is a manipulation of thought.

The Book of Proverbs is full of reassurances that the Scriptures are a tree of life to those who take hold, yet Yeshua, as well as the Older Testament prophets, remind Israel that it is possible to observe or use the Scripture for a self-serving purpose, distorting the intended light and life in its shadows of the coming Messiah.

Have you ever heard that the Torah offers "only" shadows, but the reality is in Messiah? By this many justify not studying the Torah as Words of Life, diminishing its prophetic value. It's only shadows. This is a 1) faulty proof text and 2) a logical fallacy[12]. In the presentation of the two concepts, sometimes translators can turn a phrase from the comparison

18

of two complementary ideas into adversarial ones, which is the logical fallacy called a false dilemma[13].

Consider having traffic laws *or* car insurance as opposed to having traffic laws *and* car insurance. These safeguards are not adversarial, but they work together to address safety and loss in a world of busy, distracted drivers. We appreciate one *and* the other, not one *or* the other.

A Scriptural example is John 1:17. In some translations, it reads that the Torah came through Moses, BUT grace and truth came through Messiah, and the two concepts seem at odds; however, if we more literally translate the two facts without the translator-added conjunction "but," and render the Greek more exactly, accuracy improves: "The Torah came through Moses; grace and truth was fully realized and formed [from the beginning] through Messiah."

The complementary relationship between Moses and Yeshua, Torah and grace, is easier to perceive. [14] The Torah came through Moses as a prophetic shadow of the grace and truth that is seen in the incarnate Messiah. The Torah shadowed grace and truth; it was not given as something to divert attention from the reality, but to teach about the reality. The Torah was not a diversion from grace and truth, but an accurate shadow that outlined it.

In a classroom, one learns the textbook instructions. Once students master foundational precepts, then the class can move to hands-on applications of the words. The two methods of learning are not adversarial, but complementary. The textbook study shadows the reality of the future student's expert skill in independently installing a new transmission or performing a surgery. If we are to understand the foundational work of Messiah, the Anointed One, the Righteous Branch, the Lamp of Israel, knowing what the shadows know is the due diligence of discipleship. I'm sure those who require brain surgery

13. See Dr. Robin Gould's *Colossal Controversies* for an explanation of the shadows as prophecy.

14. 13.80: to come into existence—'to be formed, to come to exist.' 'everything came into existence through him' Jn 1:3; 'before Abraham came into existence, I existed' Jn 8:58. [1] (Louw Nida 13:80; *Greek-English Lexicon of the New Testament Based on Semantic Origins*)

19

are hopeful that the surgeon is well-practiced in surgery, but they also hope that he or she started learning with the textbook instead of a saw!

Two men are mentioned as shadow pictures of the Messiah in the Book of Zechariah (3:9 KJV): Joshua and Zerubbabel. They are shadows of the Righteous Branch, and prophecy is associated with their roles:

> For behold the stone that I have laid
> before Joshua; upon one stone *shall*
> *be* **seven eyes**: behold, I will engrave
> the graving thereof, saith the LORD
> of hosts, and I will remove the iniquity
> of that land in one day.

What they knew about the seven eyes of the Holy Spirit every disciple can know. If a disciple knows the appointed times in the life of Yeshua, then he or she will listen to and understand the Word; the shadow is proof of the light.

Eye See You

Psalm 97:11 presents an interesting view of light:

> **Light is sown like seed** for the
> righteous and gladness for the
> upright in heart.

The Psalmist draws a parallel between the Light of the Word and the light separated from darkness on Day One of Creation and sprouting plants on Day Three. Light was "sown" on Day One and "grown" on Day Three. The Torah itself is Light, and the commandment is a Lamp (Psalm 6:23; 119:105). If the Light of the Torah is sown "like seed," then it is sown into darkness and emerges from darkness in a physical vessel, the "lamp." In the Creation, the trees sprouted from the darkness of the Earth on Day Three, another hint to the lamps of men, for trees are often metaphors for human beings in Scripture, such as trees of righteousness.

In like manner, it is possible to look at the entirety of the Torah as Light being sown in the Earth, and it is Israel's "charge" to care for those seven Lights in the vessels of their bodies as each one has a unique service or call. Those seven lamps are nevertheless one lamp, for in the Tabernacle instructions, Aaron was to ensure the light was cast toward the "face." This caused the light to appear as one illumination, not lamps aimed in seven different directions. It is the illuminating "face" of Adonai that is the gracious blessing of the Levitical priests.

In Hebrew, the word for eye is *ayin*, which also means a well of water.

> And I saw between the throne (with
> the four living creatures) and the
> elders a Lamb standing, as if slain,
> having seven horns and seven eyes,
> which are the seven Spirits of God,
> sent out into all the earth.[15]

The seven "eyes" of Light are seeds of Torah sown for the righteous. Moses had direct conversation with Adonai and the vision of the Tabernacle, so even though he directed the crafting of the shadows, Moses saw the reality, which so illuminated him that he had to cover his face with a veil. The removal of this veil, it says in 2 Corinthians 3:14, may be equated with seeing Yeshua as the Messiah, an embodiment of the shadow text of the Torah. The shadow is cast by a physical object standing between the earth and the direct source of the light.

In Moses' instructions, a perfect replica stood between the actual Light of the Angel of the Presence and the earth, casting the shadow we know as the Tabernacle service. Until evil men begin to distort the physical replica of grace and truth, the Tabernacle is a perfect textbook shadow

15. Re 5:6

21

of preparation for seeing the Messiah and personal practice. Every disciple's challenge is to read the Torah and to try to reconcile the shadow text with the reality of Yeshua's incarnation.

Disciples who separate the Seeds and fruits of grace and truth of the Torah from its tare distortions find that traditions and misinterpretations sometimes stand in the place of the text. Such errors cast an imperfect shadow, like the tare that at first resembles wheat, yet at maturity,[16] it will not bow the head of grain like a stalk of authentic wheat. If the Torah is the Seed, however, it is easy to see how those imperfect shadows are formed. Something has to grow from that seed, or there is nothing to see. Sown light is different from grown light, yet the same, for it grows from the authentic Seed of the Word!

Yeshua is both the authentic Seed as well as the Branch. He is the sown Light of the Torah and the grown Light of its Lamp that lights the whole world. Likewise, Yeshua's disciples are to grow light from the Seed of the Word and light the world as well[17].

The Levites could listen to or read Moses' instructions, but the details of practice would have to grow from the Seeds Moses planted in order to accurately reflect the Light of Messiah, including grace and truth. In his ministry, Yeshua spent much time clarifying how to separate a true fruit grown from the Seed of the Torah from the poisonous fruit grown from the seed of the serpent. In fact, the serpent can take a Seed principle of the Torah, twist it to serve his own purposes, and distort the picture with a deceiving shadow. The serpent's seed commandeers some aspect of the Torah Seed, and then it grows tares that only appear to be grown from the Torah until harvest time.

16. In Yeshua's parables and other passages of Scripture, harvest time is frequently a metaphor for judgment days.

For instance, the serpent deceives Eve by citing some aspects of a commandment Elohim gave her. The commandment was so that she would grow in

17. Mt 5:14; John 8:12; 9:5

22

holiness, living according to the image of Elohim [18] who created her. When the serpent offers a fruit that appears to meet that criteria, to be "wise like God," she and Adam take the bait! The little bit of truth is incorporated into a counterfeit commandment by the serpent, and with this mixture, the tare appears to be an action grown from the Seed of the Word. Just as the serpent costumed himself as a walking and talking being like a man, so his seed will appear in the costume of righteousness, frequently quoting the Word to deceive.

Although Adam was not deceived,[19] he shared in the sin; human beings are susceptible to both willful sin as well as mistaking a taredition for a tradition grown from the actual Seed of the Word. Paul writes:

> I was once alive apart from the Law; but when the commandment came, sin became alive and I died; and this commandment, which was to result in life, proved to result in death for me; for **sin, taking an opportunity through the commandment, deceived me and through it killed me**. So then, the Law is holy, and the commandment is holy and righteous and good. Therefore did that which is good become *a cause of* death for me? May it never be! Rather it was sin, in order that it might be shown to be sin by effecting my death through that which is good, so that through the commandment sin would become utterly sinful.[20]

18. Name of the Creator used in Genesis One.

19. "And it was not Adam *who* was deceived, but the woman being deceived, fell into transgression." (1 Tim. 2:14)

20. Ro 7:9–13

21. For a complete analysis of Paul's comparison between the "two men" inside of him wrestling over the Law, see *Creation Gospel Workbook Four: The Scarlet Harlot and the Crimson Thread.*

Although other BEKY Books address the greater context of this letter to the Romans,[21] what is important in the context of the commandments is that they can be used for the opposite purpose from which The Creator intended. Those who simply disregard or don't know the commandments of God are not the subject in Paul's sin teaching; those who DO know and misuse the commandments of the Torah to create sin from something designed for holy use is the subject. Paul's message in a nutshell is:

> **A holy, righteous, and good commandment can be used by sinful man to deceive a person into sinning with it instead of obeying with it!**

How can this be? Scripture documents the endless devices mankind invents to circumvent the Spiritual Eye of the Torah, such as:

- Using a commandment to appear righteous to others
- Using a commandment to command respect from others
- Using a commandment to compare one's self favorably to others
- Using a commandment merely to fulfill the letter without regard for its spiritual essence, which is to give light and to aid others
- Lending more weight to the tradition, which is a vehicle for obeying the commandment, so that it becomes more important than the commandment itself
- Replacing the actual commandment with a tradition only resembling the actual Seed of the Word, but in truth it is grown from a tare disguised as wheat; it actually violates a Seed commandment

Some of the abuses arise when a tare is substituted for the Seed of the Word, and some arise when the soil of the human heart is rocky. This is why the New Covenant in Jeremiah 31 and Ezekiel 11:19 & 36:26 included a Holy Spirit-transformed heart of flesh, not a new Seed Law. The soil was rocky, not the Seed, for the Law (Torah) of the LORD is perfect![22]

Because Eve added a "fence" around the commandment not to **eat** the fruit by stating they also were not to **touch** the fruit, some use this as a proof text that adding a barrier law to prevent someone from breaking the actual Word is what leads to the breaking of both; however, had Eve obeyed her own "rabbinic fence," it actually would have prevented her from eating the fruit. Her heart had turned rocky because of what her eyes saw.

Romans Seven defines the commandments as what reveals sin in the heart. A heart set to transgress will break all barriers put in place to prevent it, whether through deception or willful intent. If a person drives into fresh asphalt, it is not because the person was enticed to do so by a construction barrier with flashing lights and a flagman in a fluorescent orange vest. The person has either ignored all the precautions or set his heart to take a shortcut across fresh asphalt.

Things like practice (*halakha*), ritual, or custom (*minchag*) in Scripture have to grow from the Seed of the Torah, for it tells *what* to do, but not *how* to do all it commands. On the other hand, it is very clear how to do the commandment…simply *give* light as a lamp gives. Light never takes; it always gives and serves man on the earth. Something that takes light is a black hole, and that is no way to treat the Living Light and Life of the Father's perfect Word!

As Israel grew its orderly traditions, customs, practices (*takkanot* or *halakha*), and rituals, the goal was for those things to be an observable lamp: a man-plant growing good fruit from the Seed of the Torah

22. "The law of the LORD is perfect, converting the soul: the testimony of the LORD is sure, making wise the simple." (Psalm 19:7)

25

to serve mankind and glorify Adonai. This was the Father's declared purpose for His Torah, to impart light and life:

> But you who held fast to the LORD your God are **alive** today, every one of you. See, I have taught you statutes and judgments just as the LORD my God commanded me, that you should do thus in the land where you are entering to possess it. So keep and do them, for that is your wisdom and your understanding **in the sight of the peoples** who will hear all these statutes and say, 'Surely this great nation is a wise and understanding people.' For what great nation is there that has a god so near to it as is the LORD our God whenever we call on Him? Or what great nation is there that has statutes and judgments as righteous as this whole law which I am setting before you today?[23]

Numbers Eight urges order in the kindling of the menorah, the holy lamp of the Tabernacle, and order pervades the purification of the Levites and Israelite Camp movements in the wilderness. The goal of custom and practice is order within the Camp so that the lights will shine their brightest and grow good fruit. The Apostle Paul reminds gatherings of believers "Let all things be done decently and in order."[24] In context, his instructions pertain to how worship and Scripture study services should be conducted; Paul establishes local customs for the Corinthians to follow as they fulfill the Word in practice. By setting a customary order of service, Paul promotes unity. This is beneficial, for even believers in Yeshua can degenerate into endless arguments of observance that hinder the purpose of assembling to worship.

23. Deu 4:4-8

24. 1 Co 14:40

In another context, after a lengthy discussion of the more esoteric aspects of headcoverings and hair length, Paul writes to the Corinthians, "But if any man seem to be contentious, we have no such *custom*, neither the churches of God."[25] Paul identifies himself with "we," presumably Jews and Jewish believers, who have developed a custom of men wearing shorter hair than women, and therefore men are not to wear a headcover that hangs down like a woman's veil. Likewise, women customarily cover their heads when they pray or prophesy in public. Paul acknowledges that such practices are customs, not the Seed of the Word, but some investigation easily yields the Seed source of the custom: a headcover is a sign of both status and respect in the Torah[26], and cross-dressing to appear as the other sex is prohibited.

To Paul's way of thinking, it would bring order to the rowdy and formerly lascivious Corinthians to institute the Jewish customs of dress in congregational worship. Instead of drawing attention to the individual appearance, their worship would glorify the Holy One. Customs today also vary in how congregations grow orderliness from the Seed of the Word. As long as those customs direct the glory to the Father in modesty, it is good to respect that local custom, which is a Jewish principle called *minchag*.

To bear good fruit, the *Ruach HaKodesh* (Holy Spirit) must be part of the growing process, which is symbolized by the menorah in the order of the Tabernacle service. The Spirit is like that unseen, mysterious energy that makes a plant grow. In the Psalms, Prophets, and the *Brit HaChadasha* (Newer Testament), the Torah Seed words aided the Older Testament prophets and Yeshua's disciples in establishing patterns that define both good and bad trees grown from the Seed, who is Messiah, the Living Word. A good man-tree facilitates good fruit; a bad man-tree produces unripe, sour, or false fruit, like Zaccheus' false fig tree[27].

25. 1 Co 11:16

26. Priests were required to cover their heads, yet a leper was required to remove his headcover; Rebecca veiled herself when she first saw Isaac; only Nazarite men grew their hair long, which suggests an anomaly for males, and priests were required to trim their hair. These are a few examples, but there are other Seed thoughts that may apply.

27. Luke 19:4

The challenge beyond appreciating the visible shadow of truth is to define the actual Seed of the Word, a tradition grown from that seed, and a taredition. Yeshua's parable will be the guide:

> Jesus presented another parable to them, saying, 'The kingdom of heaven may be compared to a man who sowed good seed in his field. But while his men were sleeping, his enemy came and sowed tares among the wheat, and went away. But when the wheat sprouted and bore grain, then the tares became evident also. The slaves of the landowner came and said to him, "'Sir, did you not sow good seed in your field? How then does it have tares?'" And he said to them, "'An enemy has done this!'" The slaves said to him, "'Do you want us, then, to go and gather them up?'" But he said, "'No; for while you are gathering up the tares, you may uproot the wheat with them. Allow both to grow together until the harvest; and in the time of the harvest I will say to the reapers, ""First gather up the tares and bind them in bundles to burn them up; but gather the wheat into my barn.'""[28]

28. Mt 13:24–30

2

HOW A TRADITION OR A
TAREDITION GROWS FROM SEED

The Torah has many Seed commandments, but in many cases, they are terse and devoid of details. The details are left for the believing community or the individual to work out. In fact, working out the details can foster growth in the Word as one researches, prays, meditates, and seeks wise counsel.

The Jews have kept the commandments for thousands of years, and they are a people known by "Tradition...tradition!" as the song goes in *Fiddler on the Roof*. Because the Jewish people are an ethnic group formed around obedience to the Torah itself, they have ancient, numerous, and exacting methods of keeping the commandments. S. Creeger does an excellent job explaining how the Jewish sources of oral tradition emerged in *Introduction to the Jewish Sources*.

One Jewish tradition is to light two candles on Erev Shabbat to usher in the Sabbath. Nowhere in the Torah, however, is anyone commanded to light two lights for Shabbat. Why was the tradition of lighting candles or oil lamps instituted?

Contrary to what many of us might think, *hadlakat nerot* (kindling Sabbath candles) is not a mitzvah from the Torah. Before the relatively recent invention of electricity, the only source of light in each home came from a candle or an oil lamp. However, on Friday nights, since we are biblically prohibited from creating light, many Jews were left in the dark...The rabbis, in search of a solution, created a *takkanah*, decreeing that every household have two candles lit from before sunset every Friday night." (Angel, 2000)

This is easy to understand historically. Since Israel was prohibited from kindling a fire on the Sabbath[29], it was very practical to light the lamps at sundown on Friday evening so that the Israelites would have lights in all their dwellings. If the lamps are lit, then no one has to trip and fall with hands full of dishes, which would certainly spoil the peace of the Shabbat!

Why, however, in some Jewish customs is it that *two* candles are lit? The seed of Light upon which the blessing is made is found in the two Sabbath commandments in the Torah, one in Exodus 20:8 and one in Deuteronomy 5:12. Exodus commands Israel to "remember": **Zakhor** *et yom ha-shabbat le-kadesho*. To remember in Scripture is to act upon a memory, not just to retrieve a memory file from the brain. Deuteronomy commands that the Sabbath be "kept" holy: **Shamor** *et yom ha-shabbat le-kadsho*.

29. The Biblical Sabbath is from evening on Friday until evening on Saturday.

REMEMBER: KEEP

In order to reconcile the two commandments and define what it meant to remember (act) and keep (protect) the holiness of Shabbat, certain rabbis established a custom of lighting two candles, one for the act of remembering and one for the act of guarding it. The *minchag*, or local custom, of this practice may vary. Some Jews light a candle for each member of the family. Some Jews light only two, keeping a minimalistic view of the custom and the simplicity of the two commandments.

The traditional Jewish blessing is confusing for non-Jews who cannot find a commandment to light candles for Shabbat, for it reads: "Blessed are You, O Lord our God, King of the Universe, who has who has sanctified us with His commandments, and commanded us to kindle the light of the Holy Shabbat." Those who use this traditional blessing know that it is not a literal commandment to light Shabbat lights, but that the candle-lighting is the physical expression of the less tangible commandments: remember and keep. How does one "remember and keep" as a community?

Since the community agrees to light the literal Shabbat lights, then it actually IS obedience to the commandment. The commandment *defines* the Seed of obedience, but the tradition defines *how* families obey it. Is it possible to do other things to express obedience to remember and keep the Shabbat? Of course. Candle-lighting, however, is a community expression as much as an individual expression. Those who remember and keep the Sabbath stand in solidarity all over the planet lighting candles on Erev Shabbat in a very dark world. The essence of candle-lighting is for the family to BE a light to the world by obeying The Creator of the Universe.

Local practices are needed even in civil law, not just religious practice. One example from the author's personal experience is practiced by the

Federal Bureau of Prisons. The laws that govern all federal prisons are found in the Code of Federal Regulations (CFR). Each institution within the Bureau of Prisons, however, is different. There are different custody and security levels, different staff or prisoner demographics, different physical facilities, different climates, different work or educational opportunities for prisoners, and many other factors.

The rules of the CFR are very broad and often non-specific. It is up to the Bureau of Prisons to ensure that the code is enforced at every institution, so the Bureau publishes documents called Program Statements. In more detailed language, the Program Statement tells HOW every institution must meet the laws.

Since each institution is different, however, and has different resources and facilities with which to meet the requirements of the Program Statements, each local institution has Institutional Supplements, which tell in a very practical way how that particular institution will implement the corresponding Program Statement, the minimum criteria to meet the CFR.

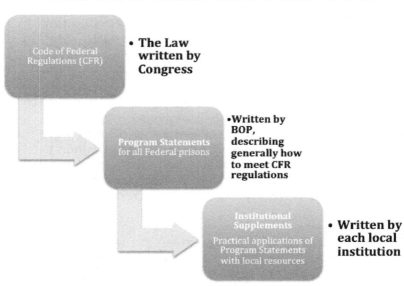

Code of Federal Regulations (CFR)

- **The Law written by Congress**

Program Statements for all Federal prisons

- **Written by BOP, describing generally how to meet CFR regulations**

Institutional Supplements

Practical applications of Program Statements with local resources

- **Written by each local institution**

This can become onerous government bureaucracy, but generally the CFR, Program Statements, and Institutional Supplements are very efficient, and they ensure that each prisoner is treated fairly. While the prisoner may not have a good relationship with a particular correctional officer, teacher, work foreman, or case manager, the presence of policies fosters humane and equal treatment of all prisoners according to set criteria, yet takes into consideration the demographics and resources of the inmate's specific institution.

In the same way that each institution operates daily on policies that aren't the actual law, but derived from it, so tradition or local custom in practicing Torah can maintain order, fairness, and a common culture of law when implemented properly. The Bureau's Program Statements and Institutional Supplements are not documents originating from nothing, but they grew from the law, the CFR. Most[30] Jewish traditions did not originate from nothing, but from Torah laws. When used according to Yeshua's instructions and examples, Jewish tradition can also maintain order in keeping the Torah and give believers a common culture.

What if there is abuse? For example, an inmate could be incarcerated in an area where he has little in common ethnically or culturally with the prison staff. Could an Institutional Supplement be written by local staff in such a way as to circumvent the CFR? It certainly could! In these cases, inmates appeal for relief up the chain of command, from the local case manager, to the warden, to the Region, and so on, until a case may be heard by the Supreme Court, which will correct the Bureau's practices or uphold them. If the Supplements or Program Statements were grown from something other than the seed of the CFR, then they are a "taredition" uprooted and rewritten to follow spirit of the law. The Bureau tries very hard to avoid the expense of lawsuits, so they expend much effort in writing Program Statements

30, A style of community dress is not a direct method of keeping the commandment, but more reflective of culture or sect. The drab garb and black hats of some Orthodox sects promote the community's perception of Seed modesty and ensure that individuals do not stand out as wealthier or poorer. Justice to the poor is a Seed, but the style of dress that is normative is custom.

and Institutional Supplements to reflect the spirit of the law.

Because it is human nature to focus on the exception or worst example of something, it is tempting to read the *Brit HaChadasha* as a book that condemns all tradition. In fact, Yeshua and his apostles at times practiced different local customs because they were from Galilee, and the Judean Jews' practices were sometimes in conflict with their own, creating religious animosity.[31] This is not unusual, for the Jewish Oral Law (*Mishnah*) records everyone's opinion in an argument, much like our modern Supreme Court. Judaism very freely looks at a question about the Torah from many angles.

Sometimes those who claim to walk scrupulously in the Word accuse others of violating the Word if they practice it differently in the practical world of custom and tradition. The advantage of studying Yeshua's judgments on questions of Law and tradition is that it gives every believer an empirical method to evaluate one's own traditions for potential abuse or circumvention of the Torah's weightier matters of justice, mercy, and faithfulness.

31. BEKY Booklet *Pharisees: Friends or Foes?* gives more details about the rival sects of First Century Judaism, but an example of the Galilean-Judean tension is recorded in John 7 where the Galileans are seen as inferior by "The Jews," which is a confusing translation, for both groups are Jewish.

One Scripture that confuses many readers is found in Colossians 2:21

> 'Do not handle, do not taste, do not touch!' (which all refer to things destined to perish with use)—in accordance with the commandments and teachings of men?

Dr. Robin Gould's *Colossal Controversies* gives a complete analysis of this passage, but the summary is that the traditions referred to by Paul in this text are the traditions of handling, tasting, and touching originating in pagan worship, the customs by which pagans were trying to judge the new converts to

Yeshua. Something that originates in pagan worship is tare, but the one holding to spiritual practices originating outside the Word doesn't know that, so they are not qualified to judge believers' observance of the commandments or traditions. This passage has nothing to do with any traditions arising from Scripture.

Even brothers and sisters in Yeshua can misjudge one another and compete for correctness, however, so if one suspects that there is a competition for correct applications afoot, a general guideline is:

> **The one trying to have the last word is rarely walking _IN_ the word.**

3

APOSTOLIC TRADITION AND JEWISH TRADITION

While it is easy to see the false dilemma of Torah vs grace and truth, another false dilemma is more difficult to discern, the "truth vs tradition" fallacy. It is easy to pronounce a tradition, ritual, pattern of worship, or custom as casting a false shadow, and some resort to denouncing all traditions and customs as antithetical to the Word. They ask, "Truth or tradition?" as if one could actually be divorced from the other. This is a false dilemma. They might say things like, "If it's not in the Torah, then it's an addition to the Torah, and that's sin!" [32] [33]

In the Prophets, Psalms, and Brit HaChadasha, however, there are lots of things added to the Torah. In some cases, the Word denounces those additions or distortions. On the other hand, customs and traditions that are grown from the Seed of the Torah for service to others are upheld. Examine the following verses:

> Now I praise you because you remember me in everything and hold firmly to the **traditions**, just as I

32. Deu 4:2; 12:32; Rev 22:18

33. "Whosoever committeth sin transgresseth also the law: for sin is the transgression of the law." (1 John 3:4 KJV)

delivered them to you.[34]

> So then, brethren, stand firm and
> hold to the **traditions** which you were
> taught, whether by word of mouth or
> by letter from us.[35]

Paul passes on traditions to the Corinthian and Thessalonian congregations in his teaching, both by word and by letters. He twice stresses that they should be held "firmly," and he praises the Corinthians for doing so. Both congregations were likely predominantly Gentile at the time of Paul's writing, so he had an expectation that all within the congregations, both Jew and Gentile, would hold and stand firmly in the traditions. In both translations of "tradition," Paul uses the Greek *paradosis*.

> Strong's Number: G3862 *Paradosis*
> Noun Feminine
>
> Definition: a giving over which is
> done by word of mouth or in writing,
> i.e. tradition by instruction, narrative,
> precept, etc.; objectively, that which
> is delivered, the substance of a
> teaching of the body of precepts,
> esp. ritual, which in the opinion of
> the later Jews were orally delivered
> by Moses and orally transmitted in
> unbroken succession to subsequent
> generations, which precepts, both
> illustrating and expanding the written
> law, as they did were to be obeyed
> with equal reverence.

The problem with these affirmations of Jewish tradition is that we don't know *which* practices Paul passed along for the congregations to grip firmly. Paul does not equate the traditions with Scripture, but he stresses their importance to the believing community. Likely it brought order within the community, and Paul did

34. 1 Co 11:2

35. 2 Th 2:15

not consider the customs as casting an imperfect shadow of the reality of Messiah Yeshua. Whatever the shadow, he felt it was a fit practice that was not sown as the seed of the serpent, but a holy Lamp to carry the Seed commandments of Light. Did Paul derive his imperative to hold the Jewish traditions from Yeshua?

> Woe to you, scribes and Pharisees, hypocrites! For you tithe mint and dill and cummin, and have neglected the weightier provisions of the law: justice and mercy and faithfulness; but these are the things you should have done without neglecting the others.[36]

In this passage, Yeshua demonstrates the nuance of growing a good Seed on bad soil! The scribes and Pharisees tithe from their herbs, an addition to the Torah, which is prohibited...or is it? If the Seed of the Torah is to tithe from grain crops and fruit, then couldn't a sincere Israelite also choose to add the tithe of even his household herb garden? In fact, Yeshua tells them they **should** have tithed from the herbs. He did not think it an addition to the Word, but a good fruit grown from the Seed to benefit the poor. So what made it a distasteful fruit?

Yeshua uses a Jewish, yet Biblical hermeneutical principle called *kal v'chomer*, or "light and heavy." A man-made tradition may be valid, but it is "lighter" in its importance than the actual Seed of the Torah, which is heavy, or "weightier." To scrupulously observe a tradition while at the same time skirting the actual justice, mercy, and faithfulness of the Seed is hypocritical[37]. Anything grown from the Seed of the Torah should be characterized by justice, mercy, and faithfulness. In the case of these particular men, the lighter tradition was observed while the heavier reality of Messiah Yeshua, the Promised Seed, was ignored.

36, Mt 23:23

37. The Greek word for "hypocrite" means an actor on a stage; one merely poses as obedient to the Word!

In another situation, Yeshua gives more clarification of *paradosis*:

> He was also saying to them, 'You are experts at setting aside the commandment of God in order to keep your tradition.' [38]

Yeshua renders three practical "tests" for a Jewish tradition (or any tradition) to assess the fruit and soil on which it is grown:

- Is the tradition grown from the Seed of the Torah, the commandments of Adonai?
- Does the one performing the custom understand its weight is lighter than those written in the Torah and that it cannot set aside the actual commandment ?
- Does the tradition grown from the Seed of the Torah have justice, mercy, and faithfulness at its heart?

A tradition observed to circumvent or break a written commandment is invalid. It is a tare also grown in bad soil, unfaithfulness. A tradition that is a vehicle for the justice, mercy, and faithfulness inherent in every commandment *is* valid. It is good fruit grown on good soil as long as it transgresses no Seed Law.

It is important not to focus too much on the actual tradition without taking a hard look at the one performing (or not performing) it. Any person who performs traditions or commandments to be seen of men and earn their respect or praise is bad soil. Not grasping that the point of any commandment or tradition is to discern the reality of Messiah Yeshua is seeing Moses through the veil. Those who view the Torah through a veil do not know what the shadows know, for the veil obstructs the Light of the Spiritual Law's reality.[39]

38. Mk 7:9

39. Ro 7:14   Yeshua's examples of the tax collector and the

40

Pharisee in prayer are another example of how one must examine the motivation of the one who practices a tradition to determine whether that custom meets Yeshua's criteria.

> And He also told this parable
> to some people who trusted in
> themselves that they were righteous,
> and viewed others with contempt:
> 'Two men went up into the temple to
> pray, one a Pharisee and the other a
> tax collector. The Pharisee stood and
> was praying this to himself: "'God,
> I thank You that I am not like other
> people: swindlers, unjust, adulterers,
> or even like this tax collector. I fast
> twice a week; I pay tithes of all
> that I get.'" But the tax collector,
> standing some distance away, was
> even unwilling to lift up his eyes to
> heaven, but was beating his breast,
> saying, "'God, be merciful to me,
> the sinner!'" I tell you, this man went
> to his house justified rather than
> the other; for everyone who exalts
> himself will be humbled, but he who
> humbles himself will be exalted.'[40]

For the non-Jewish reader, it is easy to miss the fact that both the tax collector and the Pharisee were exhibiting Jewish customs! The Pharisee boasts that he tithes of "all," not just the produce of grain, wine, oil, fruits, and livestock required in the Seed Words of the Torah. He fasts twice per week, which is not required in the Torah, but it was a custom for some Jews. The Torah only prescribes one annual fast day, Yom Kippur. It is only later in Scripture that additional community fasts are grown to commemorate significant spiritual events for the Jewish people. Yeshua describes the Pharisee's error: he may have acted as though he were praying to God, but he was praying to "himself."

40, Luke 18: 9-14

41

In his humility, the tax collector beats his breast as he requests forgiveness. Beating the breast is a Jewish custom associated with the daily Jewish *Shmonei Esrei*[41] in the *Slichah* prayer, a prayer of repentance. True gratefulness follows true repentance, and beating the breast is an ancient way to express sorrow and grief. There is a prayer of confession called the *Vidui*, in which one "puts down the head," or drops his or her head in sorrow for the sin such as the tax collector does when he prays.

Jewish customs in prayer do not promote gloating over others; the intention is to draw out heartfelt repentance and gratefulness. Humility and gratefulness are the foundation of repentance and the end result of real repentance. A heartfelt prayer *gives* the Light of the Torah; it does not shine light on the individual like the arrogant Pharisee who is violating the goal of the traditions. Although both men observe Jewish traditions grown from the Seed of the Torah, only one exemplifies how the tradition could grow the fruits of repentance. The problem was not with the tradition, but the **motivation** of the one keeping it! Good motivation is good soil. Bad motivation is rocky, dry, and shallow.

The gratefulness, humility, and forgiveness that Yeshua teaches is not grown from comparing one's self to others, but in honest self-evaluation. Statistically, envy is inversely related to gratefulness: the more one compares himself to others, the less sincerely grateful he is to his Savior for many benefits.

41. For a full explanation of the prophetic nature of the Shmoneh Esrei and an explanation of the many Names of God in it, see *Standing With Israel: a House of Prayer for All Nations* by the author.

If the tax collector was practicing an acceptable Jewish tradition of beating the breast and putting down the head in a prayer of repentance, and the Pharisee also was keeping traditions, yet using them as a point of comparison to his Jewish brother, then whether the tradition was valid was not Yeshua's point. His point, emphasized in the text, is that while one man was practicing the tradition as a reminder

42

of his own poverty of spirit, the other was practicing the tradition to misdirect the light of the Torah to himself.

If one keeps a commandment or a tradition to draw attention to his own correctness or righteousness, then his example is not one to follow, nor should any disciple learn from such a person except as an example of what NOT to do and a heart NOT to have. Comparison of interpretation, application, and practice is inevitable in learning, but maltreatment and scorn of brothers and sisters is not. Conversely, some disciples may strip themselves of all tradition and claim to follow the Torah alone, and of this they are very proud, for they believe that they have distinguished themselves from their dim brothers still caught up in the traditions of men.

What is the Seventh Abomination to The Creator that is listed Proverbs 6?

1. Not a proud look.
2. Not a lying tongue.
3. Not hands that shed innocent blood.
4. Not a heart devising wicked plans.
5. Not feet that run quickly to evil.
6. Not a false witness breathing out lies.

The Seventh Abomination, the perfection of all the previous six abominations, the abomination formed of all six abominations that preceded it is...

#7. One who separates brothers

Comparing one's self favorably to other believers

leads to arrogant separation, and Paul gives the example of his own religious zeal prior to encountering Messiah Yeshua:

> ...and I was advancing in Judaism beyond many of my contemporaries among my countrymen, being more extremely zealous for my ancestral traditions. (Galatians 1:14)

Paul explains his problem within Judaism: he was moving up the career ladder in importance. He was commandeering the traditions of his people to appear smarter, holier, and more correct in his observance. Torah Seeds were not designed for this objective, neither is the observance of any traditions grown from such a short-sighted, rocky heart.

Paul's encounter with Yeshua, however, demonstrated first how blind he was to the goal of zeal for the commandments as well as any traditions of Judaism. The point was to know the shadows so that the reality of Messiah would spring to life from the Light of the Torah. The Seed and its traditions are to bear good fruit and keep the charge of the Torah, to give Light to the earth and glorify the Father, not to take the honor and respect of men for one's self. There is nothing like temporarily losing sight to make a person appreciate vision. In his blindness, Paul finally saw the reality of Messiah and the purpose behind the heavy commandments and lighter traditions. He saw beyond the shadows.

Ironically, his encounter with Yeshua accomplished in an opposite way what Paul had sought: distinguishing himself from his countrymen. Instead of rising to the top of the Jewish Sanhedrin, Paul became the leading minister to the Gentile believers opposed by most of the leaders[42] in the Sanhedrin. Paul did not, however, forget his zeal for the traditions of his faith. He simply grew them from better soil, a new heart and life resurrected in Yeshua. For example,

42. Nicodemus was a secret follower of Yeshua until he requested the body for burial. Ironically, Peter was an open disciple until Yeshua's arrest and death, but the events brought Nicodemus into the open with the Sanhedrin and Romans. Working out our salvation is a uniquely bumpy and personal journey, but with faithfulness, we each arrive at the goal of Messiah.

Paul urges the Corinthians and Galatians:

> Now concerning the collection for
> the saints, as I directed the churches
> of Galatia, so do you also. On the
> first day of every week each one of
> you is to put aside and save, as he
> may prosper, so that no collections
> be made when I come.[43]

Paul is taking up charity (*tzedekah*) for the believers
in Jerusalem, but he does not want anyone fund-
raising while he teaches. Since the early believing
communities often met at the conclusion of Shabbat
to break bread, marking the beginning of the first
day of the week at sundown on Saturday, Paul likely
did much teaching then.[44] First Century literature
documents that believers in Yeshua continued to
attend synagogues[45] in their communities, only
later being forced to choose between church or
synagogue attendance, so this may explain their
choice of meeting time.

Jewish tradition explains why Paul would not want
anyone taking up a collection until the first workday
of the week, Sunday, for rabbinic custom prohibits
speaking of business matters or engaging in activities
that are of a distinctly weekday nature, such as
handling money, which is *muktzah*.[46] According to
Jewish law, the purpose of this tradition is to:

> ...keep Shabbat from becoming an
> ordinary weekday. (Appel, 2016, p.
> 97)

Paul is instructing his students to observe the Jewish
way of guarding Shabbat by avoiding commerce
and handling money, not to "pass the plate" during
a Shabbat service, for to do so would imply that
they had carried money to the service, which was
muktzah. These things are conducted on the other
six days of the week. The custom is very old, growing

43. 1 Co 16:1-2

44. Ac 20:7

45. Ac 15:21

46. Something
not to be
handled on the
Sabbath

45

from the Prophet Amos' exhortation:

> Hear this, you who trample the
> needy, to do away with the humble
> of the land, saying, 'When will the
> new moon be over, so that we may
> sell grain, and the sabbath, that
> we may open the wheat market,
> to make the bushel smaller and the
> shekel bigger, and to cheat with
> dishonest scales, so as to buy the
> helpless for money and the needy
> for a pair of sandals, and that we
> may sell the refuse of the wheat?' [47]

Although Jews did not handle money on Shabbat, the point of the weekly collection was to help the poor and needy of the land as Amos instructed. In the modern home, however, most believers do not live within walking distance of a Shabbat service, so accommodations are made to give tzedekah on Shabbat. Wouldn't it be wonderful if everyone kept the Shabbat so we could drop in our saved offerings any day of the week when we walked by our local congregation?

Another Jewish custom is to give tzedekah just before Shabbat on Friday afternoon, for Jewish families put aside money starting on the first day of the workweek as they were able, and it was collected it for later distribution. Modern family tzedekah boxes are periodically emptied and the contents distributed to charity.

47. Amos 8:4-6

48. For an example of tzedekah boxes crafted as beautiful works of art, see Sylvia Alotta's work at http://www.studioalotta.com

Alt-Miller (pp. 38-29) describes the family practice on Erev Shabbat just before candle-lighting. The parents set out their tzedekah box[48], and each child brings his or her own tzedekah box, which Jewish children might receive as gifts or make as a craft project. The parents pay the children their weekly allowance, and after some work to produce the proper change, each child gives 10%-20% tzedekah from his or her allowance, dropping it in the box, and the parents give tzedekah as well, for in Judaism, it is not seen as benevolence, but rather what each person owes to the poor.

This custom is grown from the Seed of the Torah, and it teaches children in a very personal way the importance of giving to the poor, expressing the heart of the Torah. After everyone has given tzedekah, the boxes are put away because no money is handled on Shabbat. The family then returns for candle-lighting, so from an early age, the children associate giving to charity with the warmth of family time at Shabbat, yet they are mindful of those who may not enjoy the same blessings.

The human factor, however, is still important. Could a child begrudge giving a portion of his allowance, and therefore diminish the Light from the tradition in his life? Of course. The heart's soil could need some work in order to grow a healthy fruit from the Seed of loving one's neighbor. This does not mean that the tradition of giving tzedekah just prior to Erev Shabbat is a taredition, but that the child's heart is in need of transformation, and this is something that good parenting can cultivate as the child grows and becomes more aware of the needs of others.

If earthly parents can cultivate the soil of a child's heart, then how much more can the Father's Ruach HaKodesh (Holy Spirit) cultivate the soil of our hearts to remember and keep the Seed from which our own traditions grow?

Mercy - Kindness or good will towards the miserable and the afflicted, joined with a desire to help them. (Greek) Zeal towards anyone, love, kindness, and pity. (Hebrew)

Faithfulness – Obedience rendered to faith; conviction of the truth of anything, belief; conviction or belief respecting man's relationship to God and divine things, generally with the included idea of trust and holy fervor born of faith and joined with it. (Greek) Faithfulness in fulfilling promises. (Hebrew)

Justice – An opinion or decision given concerning anything, esp. concerning justice and injustice, right or wrong. (Greek) What is right or just or normal, rightness, justness of weights and measures. (Hebrew)

4

THE RED SHADOW

The Torah holds the Seed words from which the rest of the Older Testament (TANAKH) and Newer Testament grow. Those books of Scripture between Joshua and Revelation document traditions grown from the Torah. In fact, even the Torah seeds the idea that customs will grow from the Torah itself:

> Therefore, to this day the sons of
> Israel do not eat the sinew of the hip
> which is on the **socket** of the thigh,
> because he touched the socket of
> Jacob's thigh in the sinew of the hip.
> [49]

This ancient battle between Esau and Jacob is a Seed pattern demonstrating both the struggle of mankind and the practice of traditions to preserve the memory of a Seed event in the Torah.

The sensitive areas of both the foot and the hand are symbolic in Scripture. The foot, specifically the heel, represents the soul. In Hebrew, the soul is the *nefesh*. The shortest definition of the soul is a bundle of appetites, emotions, desires, and intellect. The heel becomes very hard and calloused, but the sole (Hebrew: *caph*) remains highly sensitive. When

49. Gen 32:32

Jacob is born, he is holding onto red, hairy Esau's heel, pointing to the place of Esau's vulnerability, his appetites. The heel is the point of vulnerability to Eve's "seed," yet the point of vulnerability to the serpent-beast is the head, the symbol of the spirit.

In his appetite for the "red stuff" and Canaanite women, Esau is both hardened predator and vulnerable prey, like a beast. He hunts for game and that which pleases his soul, and this is exactly how Jacob deceives his father Isaac out of Esau's blessing and bargains with Esau for his birthright in Genesis 25. His soul appetites were what made Esau the prey, for all that is needed to bait a Red One like Esau is food, the hunt (competition), sexual pleasure, emotional pleasure, or intellectual achievement. Being governed by these desires instead of mastering them with the Spirit are the beast's vulnerabilities.

Esau[50] represents the red stuff, a rowdy soul seeking pleasure and achievement. When Jacob returns to the Land to face Esau, he struggles one night with a "man," whom he declares has the face of God, and Jacob names the place of the wrestling match Peniel. This struggle resulted in Jacob being smitten in the thigh socket, the caph[51].

Before Jacob could face his twin Esau, he had to wrestle the Esau within. Jacob[52] was notorious for relying on his own heel, which in Jacob's case, was the hardened intellect of his soul, to obtain the result he wanted. Jacob, too, needed for his spirit to prevail over his red soul in order to conquer Red One within, for this is a competition worth winning. It changed Jacob's walk to do so, as it will any disciple's walk when he practices walking after the Spirit instead of his soul. When a disciple walks in the Spirit, it is with the sensitivity of the sole of his foot to the Spirit, not the vulnerability to his red desires.[53]

In Revelation Three, the fifth assembly is Sardis. It literally means "Red Ones." In rabbinic tradition,

50. Esau's nickname in Scripture is Edom, the Red One, from adom, which means red in Hebrew.

51. Caph in Hebrew denotes things with a cup-like structure, like the palm of the hand, the sole of the foot, or the thigh socket. The Jewish male headcover is called a kippah, for its cuplike structure resembles the cupping of a hand on the head to ordain, bless, or consecrate. Caphar means atonement, from which comes the word for the appointed time of Yom Kippur, the Day of Atonement. Leviticus 14:18 is a good example of the overlapping themes of caph and caphar.

Esau (Edom) is the Red One, for he was born red and hairy all over like a beast, and Esau's Biblical nickname Edom comes from *adom*, or the color red. The Sardinians are singled out as conforming to the image of the hairy beast Esau, a man controlled by his appetites. The Seed of the Torah hints to the principle of the first born beast, for in Day Six of Creation, the beast was created first, yet the second-born man was created to rule over the beasts, for the man was made in the image of Elohim, who is Spirit.

When he walks into to his father's tent not knowing that Jacob has already deceived his way to the blessing, Esau tells his father, "I am your **firstborn**, Esau." Because his father Isaac has been deceived through his own red soul, his vulnerable appetite for wild game, the Red One Esau is right on target. Isaac began his walk with the God of his father Abraham by sowing seed in the field and reaping a hundredfold, yet at a critical time of rendering the blessing to the firstborn, Isaac is vulnerable to the appetites of a man who hunts in the field instead of sowing seed in it! These are critical links between the serpent, the most cunning beast of the field (Gen. 3:1) and the man of the field, Esau (Gen. 25:27).

Each of the seven assemblies in the Book of Revelation correspond to a *moed*, or feast day, listed in the Torah.[54] The assembly at Sardis is the easiest example of the seven, for several phrases, idioms, and traditions relative to Rosh HaShanah, the Feast of Trumpets, establish that Yeshua's message to Sardis is almost word-for-word a collection of Jewish tradition on the feast. Were all those Jewish traditions gleaned from the scarce Seeds in the Torah?

While there may be some Jewish traditions of uncertain origin, the Scriptures uphold the traditions of Rosh HaShanah in Revelation, so we can be sure they're grown from good Seed, and if the Red Ones are willing to repent of their poor motivations, then fruit will grow from good soil, a clean heart, good

52. Jacob in Hebrew is *Yaakov*, commonly translated as "supplanter," but the root *ekev* refers to the heel or that which comes after.

53. For a thorough study into the spirit, soul, body, and the Esau/Jacob symbols, see the author's *Creation Gospel Workbook Four: The Scarlet Harlot and the Crimson Thread*.

54. See Appendix D for a summary of each feast or *Creation Gospel Workbook One: The Creation Foundation* for a complete explanation of the Seven Churches of Revelation as the Seven Feasts of Adonai listed in the Torah.

fruit from good Seed.

Rosh HaShanah initiates the Fall season of feasts in the Torah. Examine each statement from Revelation 3:1-6 addressed to the Red Ones below, and a shadow Seed from the Torah explains from where the Jewish tradition may have grown.

> To the angel of the church in Sardis write: He who has **the seven Spirits of God** and the **seven stars**, says this: 'I know your deeds, that you have a name that you are **alive, but you are dead.**'

Torah Seed: A traditional Jewish Torah portion begins in Numbers 8:1 with the seven-branched menorah, representing the Seven Spirits of God and the seven assemblies. The [chiastic] middle of the seven days of Creation is the fourth, the day when the stars were placed to witness to the *moedim*[55] (feasts).

Jewish tradition: Deeds are examined each year from Rosh HaShanah to Yom HaKippur. Figuratively, the dead one resurrects from the deeds of the past year in order to navigate the path that the Father has decreed for him in the coming year. As he hears the sound of the shofar[56] /trumpet on Rosh HaShanah, the repentant one dies (sleeps) and is resurrected "in the twinkling of an eye." This is exactly what Paul teaches his Gentile converts:

> Behold, I tell you a mystery; we will not all sleep, but we will all be changed, in a moment, in the twinkling of an eye, at the last trumpet; for the trumpet will sound, and the dead will be raised imperishable, and we will be changed.[57]

55. Gen 1:14

56. ram's horn blown like a trumpet

The "last trump" is the trumpet of Rosh HaShanah,

and the "great trump" is sounded ten days later at Yom Kippur.

The pillar of cloud arose for travel in the wilderness, guiding the Israelites along the pre-determined path. The pattern of rising is one theme embedded in Jewish Rosh HaShanah tradition of the greater resurrection from the dead. Significantly, the Sardinians are told to "Wake up, and strengthen the things that remain, which were about to die; for I have not found your deeds completed in the sight of My God." Jewish tradition connects the deeds of the past and the coming years with repentance, death, and resurrection:

> A widespread Ashkenazic practice is for men to wear a white cloak called a kittel on Yom Kippur. Sefer Ra'avyah (no. 528) explains that on Yom Kippur, we resemble angels. Wearing a kittel reflects our spiritual purity in this elevated state. Rema (Shulchan Arukh, Orah Hayyim 610:4), on the other hand, avers that the kittel resembles **a shroud. The image of death should jolt one into repentance.** (Angel, M. 2000, p. 43)

Torah Seed: The act of waving of a wave offering in Numbers Eight is an "elevation"[58] that shadows resurrection from something old to something new. The Levites even shaved all their body hair before their elevation, symbolically returning to a newborn state and immersing in water like a womb for their dedication to service in the House.

Jewish tradition: The completion of each year's circuit is the time to examine one's self for success or failure in navigating the prescribed path. As the person has aged through the year, he dies and is resurrected on Rosh HaShanah. The good lives on, but the Red One's transgressions should die as the

57. 1 Co 15:51–52

58. You can hear the root of *alah,* for "going up" (Strong's #5927) in the title of the Torah portion *Behaalotkha* (Numbers 8:1-12:16); it means to ascend, to climb, or to sprout forth like vegetation. The menorah was crafted with almond blossoms, demonstrating the Ruach's (Holy Spirit's) resurrection power.

believer confesses his sins[59]. A common saying at Rosh HaShanah is "Awake you sleeper, arise from the dead." In the words of the Rambam[60], the shofar calls out, "Awaken you sleepers from your (spiritual) slumber. Search out your ways and return to Hashem [God] in Teshuva [repentance]."

This resurrection tradition of the Fifth Feast, the Feast of Trumpets/Rosh HaShanah, is chiastic[61] to the Third Feast, Firstfruits of the Barley, and Firstfruits is also a resurrection day, coinciding with the day that Yeshua and the righteous saints of old resurrected from the dead.[62] Telling the Red Ones of the Fifth Church to "strengthen the things that remain" is a hint to the Fifth Spirit of Adonai, *Gvurah*, or Strength (see Appendix A).

On the Fifth Day of Creation, Elohim creates the birds and fish. In the prophetic shadow of the Torah portion Seed, the rabble crave free *fish* like they had in Egypt, and Adonai gives them *birds* to eat until they come out of their noses. Moses is skeptical, asking if all the fish of the sea were gathered, would it be enough? The Israelites complained of the manna that "parched" their souls, but the chiastic resurrection-mate of Sardis is Pergamum, which is promised "hidden manna"[63] if they overcome their parched souls with what the Spirit said. If Israel's flesh and soul appetites could be ruled by spiritual appetites, then resurrection could occur as the Bread of Life taught.

> So **remember** what you have received and heard; and keep it, and repent. Therefore if you do not wake up, I will come like a thief, and **you will not know at what hour I will come to you**.

Torah Seed: Rosh HaShanah is a *moed* of remembrance, as detailed in the Seed Torah portion:

59. 1 John 1:9

60. Maimonides, a respected Jewish scholar

61. See Appendix A, a graphic of the menorah. A chiasm occurs when two sides become a mirror of the other. If the menorah were folded at its middle, then the third and fifth days would touch; since both emerge from the same "bud" location on the central trunk of the menorah, they share the same theme, resurrection.

62. Mt 27:53

63. Yeshua identifies himself as the Bread from Heaven, identifying both as the manna hidden with the commandments in the Ark of the Covenant and the Word hidden with the Father until he was sent to feed Israel.

On a day of your gladness, on your festivals, and your new moons, **you shall sound the trumpets** over your **elevation-offerings** and over your peace-offerings; and **they shall be a remembrance** for you before your God. (10:10)

The blasts are associated specifically with *olah* (elevation) offerings of resurrection and the beginning of the months; Rosh HaShanah is a double celebration, for it is both the first of the month, the turn of the year, and the Day of Blowing. Although many think the traditional Jewish nickname for the Feast of Trumpets, Rosh HaShanah, is a misnomer because it is not called by this name specifically in the Torah, there is a textual link to its function.

Rosh HaShanah[64] means "Head (Beginning) of the Year" in Hebrew, but the Torah Seed calls it Yom Teruah, the Day of Blowing [the trumpets]. At first glance, this supplants the Seed with a tare, but does it? *Shanah* in Hebrew is more than a year; it is a change. A year marks a change, so it is a play-on words that Paul renders for his non-Jewish readers to understand:

> Behold, I tell you a mystery; we will not all sleep, but **we will all be changed**, in a moment, in the twinkling of an eye, at the last trumpet; for the trumpet will sound, and the dead will be raised imperishable, and **we will be changed.**[65]

Rosh HaShanah is the beginning of the change. What change? It is an agricultural and spiritual change of the year. The crops are gathered in, like the Body of Messiah at the Feast of Trumpets, yet they are transformed to new life in resurrection. Is there a Torah Seed to confirm this, or was Paul mistaken?

64. The Babylonian new year *Akitu* fell on the 1st day of Tishrei, which coincided with Yom Teruah on the 1st day of the Seventh Month. When Jews in captivity started calling the Seventh Month by the Babylonian name Tishrei, the rabbis did not want it confused with the pagan new year, so they added the name Rosh Hashanah to Yom Teruah, which eventually became the more common name for this holiday. Shanah's root means a change or transformation, *shinui*. (Ganor, 2016) The transformational theme of Yom Teruah distinguished the Jewish change of the year from Akitu.

65. 1 Co 15:51–52

Torah Seed:

> You shall celebrate the Feast of Weeks, that is, the first fruits of the wheat harvest, and **the Feast of Ingathering at the turn of the year.** [66]

> Also you shall observe the Feast of the Harvest of the first fruits of your labors from what you sow in the field; also the Feast of the Ingathering **at the end of the year** when you gather in the fruit of your labors from the field.[67]

> Then Moses commanded them, saying, "**At the end** of every seven years, at the time of the year of remission of debts, at the Feast of Booths…[68]

> You are also to count off seven sabbaths of **years** for yourself, seven times seven **years**, so that you have the time of the seven sabbaths of **years**, namely, forty-nine **years.** You shall then sound a ram's horn abroad on the tenth day of the **seventh month**; on the day of atonement you shall sound a horn all through your land.[69]

66. Ex 34:22. The word translated "turn" is *tekufah*: turn or circuit

67. Ex 23:16 The word translated as "end" is *yatza*, the going out, exit

68. Deu 31:10 The word translated as "end" is *ketz*, end

69. Lev 25:8-9 This blowing of the ram's horn declares the year of Jubilee when all landholders in Israel return to their land

70. Ex 12:2

While the first month of the year occurs in the spring, the month of Passover,[70] the fall feasts of Trumpets, the Day of Atonement, and Tabernacles mark the end *and* the beginning of a year…in the seventh month. To the Western mind that is conditioned to demand either/or, true or false, this is mind-blowing!

It is no different, however, than looking into the sky and seeing two luminaries: the sun by day, and the moon by night. Each serves a similar, but separate function in keeping the Earth in livable balance, but they are not in conflict with the purpose of the other. [71] The sun determines the years, but the moon determines a month.

Seeing a Passover slain lamb seated on the Rosh HaShanah living King's throne is not a conflict. A new year of freedom in the Fall does not conflict with the beginning of months in the Spring, and thankfully, both seasons offer prophecies of resurrection in Messiah Yeshua. In fact, the themes of the feasts overlap one another, so they are different, yet they are one, just as the menorah is one piece of beaten gold.

Jewish Tradition: The Sardinians were warned that judgment day would come upon them like a thief if they did not awake. In Jewish tradition, judgment day is Yom Kippur, the Day of Atonement, yet it begins ten days earlier at Rosh HaShanah to awake the "dead" sleeper with a trumpet in time to prepare his garments for resurrection to life instead of leaving them stained for harsh judgment. With Yeshua's advocacy for us with the Father, there is no reason to be caught sleeping, dead in trespass and sin, nor to awaken with stained garments.

There is a Jewish idiom for that awakening day, Rosh HaShanah: "The day and the hour that no man knows..." It may be an allusion to the movement of the cloud in the Torah Seeds of Exodus. Even Moses didn't appear to know, for he also had to wait for the cloud. "And whenever the cloud was lifted from atop the Tent, afterwards the Children of Israel would embark...Sometimes the cloud...for a number of days...sometimes remain...or for a day and a night... or for two days, or a month or a year..." (selected from among 9:15-23).

Torah Seeds: The Sardinians are cautioned how to prepare for a time of tribulation on earth such

71. For an excellent overview of the new moon relative to feast observance and the beginning of the new month and spiritual renewal, see Kisha Gallagher's *The Biblical New Moon: A Beginner's Guide for Celebrating.*

as has never been seen before. The work of the beast and the dragon will grow intense, and they will make war against the Woman's children who keep the commandments of God and the testimony of Yeshua. To prepare for such an enemy, Exodus 10:9 commands: "When you go to war in your land against the adversary who attacks you, then you shall sound an alarm (*teruah*-shout) with the trumpets, that you may be remembered before the LORD your God, and be saved from your enemies." The shout of the *teruah* causes Adonai to remember them and scatter their enemies.

Jewish tradition: Rosh HaShanah is celebrated as the "day and hour that no man knows" and the "day of the awakening blast," and it is celebrated for two days as a precaution because of the lack of certainty in sighting the new moon marking the date. The *teruah* (shout), *tekiah* (clap), and *shvareem* (wail), are the shofar or horn blasts marking the synagogue services, which are marked by prayers of repentance.

The *tekia* blast of Rosh HaShanah crowns Adonai as King. The long, straight shofar blast is the sound of the King's coronation. *Shvareem* is three wailing, medium blasts resembling the keening/ululation commonly heard in the Middle East both as a celebration sound and a wailing, mourning sound. It demonstrates grief for the shortcomings of the previous year and Israel's recognition of the need for repentance. The *teruah*, which is nine quick blasts, is an alarm clock, arousing Israel from spiritual slumber to seek clarity, alertness, and focus.

The Talmud of Jewish oral law says when there's judgment from below, there's no need for judgment from above. If Jews examine themselves for how they've fallen short in the past and what they expect to change in the future, then there is no need to "wake up" to what is already perceived and sacrificed on the altar of repentance.

> But you have a few people in Sardis
> who have not soiled their garments;
> and they will walk with Me in white,
> for they are worthy.

Torah Seeds: The "few" people in Sardis are representative of the Levites (8:5; 14-19) chosen as redemption in place of the firstborn of the "legions" of the tribes, all listed with their banners and leaders in Chapter Ten. Because they stood with Moses against the worshippers of the Golden Calf, they were worthy of the priesthood (Exodus 32:25-29). The white garments of the dedicated priesthood are in 8:21 and Exodus 28.

Jewish tradition: White garments traditionally are worn in the synagogue on the first day of Rosh HaShanah.

> He who overcomes will thus be
> **clothed in white garments**; and I will
> not **erase his name from the book
> of life**, and I will confess his name
> before My Father and before His
> angels.

Torah Seeds: In 8:7, Adonai commands that the Levites wash their garments, "and they shall become pure." In Exodus 8:6, Moses literally clothes Aaron in the priestly garments. The white garments were to be worn in the Holy of Holies beyond the veil rather than the High Priest's colorful, royal attire.

In Exodus 32:32, Moses begs Adonai not to take His Presence from Israel, for he would rather have his own name blotted out of the Book along with his brothers and sisters, even in their failures.

Jewish tradition: New garments are worn at Rosh HaShanah. White is the tradition on the first day, and then any color but red on the second day. In some Middle Eastern communities, such as the Baghdadi, white clothes and shoes were also worn at Shavuot, not just Rosh HaShanah and Yom Kippur (Yerushalmi, 2007, Loc. 1754 of 3932).

The Rosh HaShanah/Yom Kippur tradition of judgment from the Books is detailed in the Jewish oral law, Mishnah Rosh Hashana 16b, and echoed, in different words, by the Jewish sage Rambam, Hilchos T'shuvah 3:3.

> He who has an ear, **let him hear** what the Spirit says to the churches.

Torah Seed: In Chapter Ten, Moses is commanded to craft two silver trumpets to summon the assembly and signal when the camps were to move. To ignore the trumpets would result in being left behind. Behind left behind should not happen to anyone who keeps the Feast of Trumpets at its appointed time! The teruah blast was to move the Camp to action: "But when you blow an alarm, the camps that are pitched on the east side shall set out…" In Hebrew, the *teruah* also can mean a shout.

Jewish tradition: Hearing the sound of the shofar is the primary commandment of Rosh HaShanah.

Paul in 1 Thessalonians 4: 13-18 uses traditional Jewish themes of Rosh HaShanah to illustrate the return of Yeshua from the shadow seeds of Torah:

> But we do not want you to be uninformed, brethren, about those who are asleep, so that you will not grieve as do the rest who have no hope. For if we believe that Jesus died and rose again, even so God will bring with Him <u>those who have fallen asleep in Jesus</u>. For this we say to you **by the word of the Lord**, that **we who are alive and remain until the coming of the Lord, will**

not precede those who have fallen asleep.

Torah Seed: In the Chapter Twelve finale of *Behaalotkha* is the infamous incident of Aaron and Miriam speaking out about the Cushite woman. In some Jewish literature, it is posited that Miriam was not speaking against the Cushite, but against Moses for withdrawing from conjugal relations with his wife due to his responsibilities. When the cloud departed, Miriam was put outside the Camp with leprosy, which Aaron equates with her being born dead. Figuratively, Miriam is dead outside the Camp and the Presence has withdrawn, causing Aaron and Moses to cry out on her behalf. Neither the cloud nor the Camp moves until she is restored after seven figurative days of death.

Jewish tradition: Death is viewed as "sleep" in Rosh HaShanah literature. Paul writes to the Thessalonians that those who are asleep in Messiah are not without hope, possibly pointing to the strong intercession of Moses and Aaron on behalf of Miriam. Both Moses the lawgiver and Aaron the Light-bringer pray for restoration so that the **entire** Camp may once again move. Miriam's resurrection from the dead preceded the gathering of "living" Israel into the clouds for forward movement.

> For **the Lord Himself will descend from heaven with a shout**, with the voice of the **archangel and with the trumpet of God**, and the dead in Christ will rise first.[72]

> God has **ascended** with a **shout**, the LORD, **with the sound of a trumpet**. [73]

Torah Seeds: It was the Lord Himself, the Angel of the Presence, who descended in the cloud to speak with Moses; the Name was in Him to heal and to forgive

72. 1 Th 4:16

73. Ps 47:5

61

sins.   When Aaron and Miriam spoke against the Cushite, "The LORD descended in a pillar of cloud and stood at the entrance to the Tent of Meeting..." (12:5).

> But when you blow an alarm (teruah-shout), the camps that are pitched on the east side shall set out.

Jewish tradition: The pillar descended, but when it was time to ascend, a shout signaled that the people were to move with His Presence.   Jewish tradition affirms the rest of Paul's exhortation to the Thessalonians: "Then we who are alive and remain will be caught up together with them in the clouds to meet the Lord in the air, and so we shall always be with the Lord."

Torah seed:

> And whenever the cloud was lifted from atop the Tent, afterwards the Children of Israel would embark, and in the place where the cloud would rest, there the Children of Israel would encamp. Sometimes the cloud...for a number of days... sometimes remain...or for a day and a night...or for two days, or a month or a years... (selected from among 9:15-23).

> The cloud was over them by day when they journeyed from the camp. When the Ark would travel, Moses would say, 'Arise, HaShem, and let Your foes be scattered, let those who hate You fell from before You.' And when it rested, he would say, 'Return, HaShem, to the myriad thousands of Israel" (10:34-35 *Artscroll* TANAKH).

The return of "the Lord Himself" in the letter to the Thessalonians parallels the movement of the cloud/ ark in the wilderness. The movement of the cloud was matched by the movement of the Ark carrying the Word of God.

Jewish tradition: The cloud/Word scattered the enemy, and then it returned to the myriad thousands of Israel, which matches Paul's description of the gathering of the saints. The cloud of the Angel of the Presence was centered at the "Tent of Meeting,"[74] suggesting it as the standard and rallying point for all Israel in the resurrection.

The Greek word *aer* translated "in the air" in 1 Thessalonians Four refers to breathable air close to the earth. It does not imply clouds high above the earth. This is congruent with the Jewish tradition that the Israelites walked in "clouds of glory" in the wilderness, for from the many passages about the movement of the cloud in the wilderness and the initial camp at Sukkot, they derive that Israel entered into Sukkot (Tabernacle) clouds of glory when they exited Egypt.

Who was at the forefront of the Camp's movement? Judah. After the Babylonian exile, any of the tribes who still had their tribal identity called themselves "Jews." Could this arrangement be a Torah shadow-Seed from which the plant and fruit of Jewish leadership in the Shabbat, the moedim, and Temple services grows?

> Behold, on the mountains the feet of him who brings good news, who announces peace! Celebrate your feasts, **O Judah**; pay your vows. For never again will the wicked one pass through you; he is cut off completely. [75]

Then the word of the LORD of hosts

74. The Tabernacle was also called the *Ohel Moed*, or Tent of Appointed Time, a reference to the moedim, the feasts of Adonai during which all Israel gathered to worship.

came to me, saying, 'Thus says
the LORD of hosts, "'The fast of the
fourth, the fast of the fifth, the fast of
the seventh and the fast of the tenth
months will become joy, gladness,
and cheerful feasts for the **house of
Judah**; so love truth and peace…
It will yet be that peoples will come,
even the inhabitants of many cities.
The inhabitants of one will go to
another, saying, ""'Let us go at once
to entreat the favor of the LORD,
and to seek the LORD of hosts; I will
also go.'"" So many peoples and
mighty nations will come to seek
the LORD of hosts in Jerusalem and
to entreat the favor of the LORD…
In those days ten men from all the
nations will grasp **the garment of
a Jew**, saying, 'Let us go with you,
for we have heard that God is with
you.'[76]

Then what advantage has **the
Jew**? Or what is the benefit of
circumcision? Great in every
respect. First of all, that they were
entrusted with the oracles of God.
[77]

…who are Israelites, to whom
belongs the adoption as sons, and
the glory and the covenants and the
giving of the Law and the temple
service and the promises…[78]

75. Nah 1:15   Judah is at the forefront of the Camp's movement,
76. Zec 8:19-23   and according to Nahum, Zechariah, and Paul, they
also are charged with the primary responsibility of
77. Ro 3:1-2   safeguarding both the prescribed weighty moedim
as well as any "lighter" additional fasts or feasts of
78. Ro 9:4-5   tradition. Zechariah does not object to Judah's

addition of fast days to Yom Kippur, rather, by describing how they will be transformed to joy for all nations[79] in Messiah's reign, Zechariah validates as helpful what some may judge a taredition to the Torah. What Judah grew from the seed of the Torah was a good tradition that foreshadowed Israel's resurrection life in Messiah.

79. Even the Assembly at Laodicea [see Appendix A] in Revelation holds Jewish tradition, which assigns the scales of justice as a theme of the month of Tishrei, the Seventh Month. Laodicea means "justice of the peoples."

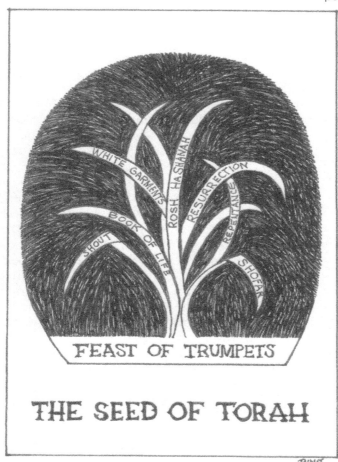

FEAST OF TRUMPETS

THE SEED OF TORAH

It would be a grave mistake to elevate Jewish traditions above the Torah, which casts the perfect shadow; however, to completely disregard Jewish tradition would be to lose the context of much of Scripture, especially the Newer Testament, which teaches a transformed heart, not a transformed Torah. Without any frame of instructional reference for observance, practice in a Torah walk can become increasingly bizarre as the learner remains blind to the movement of the Camp led by Judah... who was led of the Angel of the Presence. This is both a Seed and shadow of the reality in the Lion of Judah. The result of total disregard for Judah's scepter is family division, unceasing arguments, and wayward disunity.

While there may be some unfathomable traditions, fables, or customs within Judaism,[80] exercise caution in the daily walk. The body of Jewish oral law has increased exponentially since the First Century believers were educated in some of the customs, so gathering a body of believers is a challenge when so many despair of finding the "right," "correct," or "truthful" methods of observance.

This is a transition generation just like the First Century, a generation in which it is possible to put faith in Yeshua as the Messiah as well as to faithfully observe the Father's commandments. Abiding in the cloud and with the crowd can be a challenge, especially when at the extremes some have fallen in love with anything Jewish, while others abhor anything "rabbinic." Take His Hand, Yeshua, the authority. Keep an eye on Judah for movement and rest times in order to stay in and under the cloud. The Levites gather,[81] and Judah is the royalty of covering authority. Avoid tareditions, but don't label as sin Jewish traditions grown from the Seed and good soil.

At the command of the LORD they remained encamped, and at the command of the LORD they

80. The Jewish sages do not attempt to rationalize all of the rabbinic laws, for the "motivation in enacting laws was to protect the laws of the Torah. As a general rule, Chazal (the sages) did not make laws to protect other rabbinic laws... it does not mean that gezerot do not have an internal logic and mechanism. Therefore, while the ultimate motivation for the gezerah is to protect a Torah law, the result of the gezerah may affect actions that would be seemingly disconnected from protecting Torah law." (Appel, 2016, p. 97)

journeyed; they kept the charge
of the LORD, at the command of
the LORD by the hand of Moses.
(Numbers 9: 23)

So they departed from the mountain
of the LORD on a journey of three
days; and the ark of the covenant
of the LORD went before them for
the **three days' journey**, to **search
out a resting place for them**. And the
cloud of the LORD was above them
by day when they went out from the
camp. (Numbers 10:33-34)

It is a three-day journey to rest, and the three days
were a symbol to which Yeshua repeatedly alluded.
The gathering at the Passover season on the third
feast, Firstfruits, is a first resurrection. Will we walk
in the clouds from the Day of the Awakening Blast
to Sukkot? Yeshua is the Angel of the Presence in
the cloud, and he is covering, clothing, speaking to,
and resurrecting Israel. That same Hand is judging
those on the earth who are weighed in the balances
and found wanting. Clouds make a shadow in the
earth on a sunny day, but the sun does not make
clear shadows in the day of darkness. Instead, the
reality is found in Messiah, who is in the cloud with his
witnesses.

The shadows know.

81. Levi's birth
order is a hint.
His birth order of
third corresponds
to the Third Day
when the waters
were gathered,
signifying his
Levitical role
in gathering
Israel to the
Tent of Meeting.
Immersion and
sprinkling with
water is a vital
part of the
Levitical rituals
in the books of
Leviticus and
Numbers. The
firstborn Reuben
is described as
"unstable as
water," like the
chaos of the
deep on Day
One.

5

WOW, THAT'S JEWISH?

As with the Jewish idioms and expectations in the message to Sardis, there are many passages in the Brit HaChadasha that have origins in Jewish tradition, scholarship, and idiom. There are so many that it would be impossible to list all of them in a booklet. A few of the more obvious ones assist the non-Jewish reader in appreciating the rich Jewish heritage of the writers of the Gospels, Epistles, and even the Revelation of John.

The Very Appearance of Evil

If the reader of Scripture has always assumed that Paul was anti-rabbinic, then his statement in Acts 23:6 sounds strange at best, and disingenuous at worst:

> But perceiving that one group were
> Sadducees and the other Pharisees,
> Paul began crying out in the Council,
> 'Brethren, I am a Pharisee, a son of
> Pharisees; I am on trial for the hope
> and resurrection of the dead!'

While admittedly Paul was clever as well as learned, he was signaling something important to his accusers and those listening. He identified with the teachings of the Pharisees, specifically, the Pharisaic School of Hillel. A detailed explanation of why this is important may be found in the BEKY Book, *Pharisees: Friends or Foes?* In this context, however, Paul distinguishes himself from the Sadducees who rejected Jewish traditions, particularly Jewish Oral Law as developed by the two Pharisaic schools of Hillel and Shammai.

The Sadducees were not void of tradition, but their beliefs and practices were focused on the written Torah, while the Pharisees devoted much effort to the Jewish Oral Law. As Paul cites, the Pharisees believed in the resurrection of the dead, not the most obvious of Torah concepts, but definitely in the Spirit of the Torah and the Jewish Oral Law. The Sadducees took the most literal views of Scripture, denying the resurrection of the dead.

In I Thessalonians 5:22-23, Paul writes:

> Abstain from all appearance of evil.
>
> And the very God of peace sanctify you wholly; and I pray God your whole spirit and soul and body be preserved blameless unto the coming of our Lord Jesus Christ.

Did Paul simply generate these ideas from personal study, or did he learn them in a school of the Pharisees? In the Jewish Oral Law is a principle called *Mar'it Ha'ayin*, which is defined in *The Concise Code of Jewish Law*: "The prohibition of an act because of the appearance of wrongdoing." (Appel, 2016, p.99) The "fence" of the (rabbinic) prohibited act itself might not be prohibited in the Word, yet it could lead to a Torah-prohibited act or be misconstrued by others, allowing them to stumble into sin. The extra fence ensured that the Name of God would not be profaned by misconduct.

This aspect of Jewish Oral Law is based on Numbers 32:22: "You shall be clean before the Lord **and** before Israel."

I Corinthians 8:9-12 also demonstrates Paul's rabbinic training:

> But take care that this liberty of yours does not somehow become a stumbling block to the weak. **For if someone sees you**, who have knowledge, dining in an idol's temple, **will not his conscience, if he is weak, be strengthened to eat things sacrificed to idols?** For through your knowledge he who is weak is ruined, the brother for whose sake Christ died. And so, by **sinning against the brethren** and wounding their conscience when it is weak, **you sin against Christ**.

Paul mentions some key elements from both the actual Torah prohibition and the Jewish Oral Law. First, someone might see an act and misconstrue it as a violation of the Torah, specifically against idol worship and eating things sacrificed to idols. Paul prohibits believers from eating within the precincts of a pagan temple so that the uninformed or "weak" onlooker does not construe this as actually participating in a pagan ritual eating act and believe that it is okay to eat pagan sacrifices. Even though believers know that idols are mute and impotent, the weaker believer may not be as firm in his faith, relying on the example of others to learn and form his practices.

Secondly, Paul relates sinning against the weaker brother to sinning against Messiah. By avoiding the very appearance of evil, or *ma'arit ha'ayin*, the stronger believer acts in faith toward his brother Israelites, which makes him clean before God **and** men. This is a process of sanctification in one's faith, and this principle of Jewish Law gives definition to what it means to be clean before God *and* men in Numbers 32:22.

For the Sake of the Gentiles[82]

Most Christians are familiar with Paul's rationale for the majority of First Century Jews' rejection of Yeshua as Messiah:

> I say then, they did not stumble so as to fall, did they? May it never be! But by their transgression salvation has come to the Gentiles, to make them jealous. Now if their transgression is riches for the world and their failure is riches for the Gentiles, how much more will their fulfillment be![83]

> For I do not want you, brethren, to be uninformed of this mystery—so that you will not be wise in your own estimation—that a partial hardening has happened to Israel until the fullness of the Gentiles has come in; and so all Israel will be saved...(v. 25-26)

Where did Paul get the idea that there was a master plan behind this phenomenon? In the Jewish Oral Law (Pesachim 87b), it is stated, "The Jewish people were exiled from the Land of Israel only for the sake of the *gerim* (strangers) who would be added to them." (Ben Avraham, 2012, pp. 57, 161) While traditional Jewish expectation did not specifically include Yeshua's death and resurrection as part of the First Century events that led to the destruction of the Temple, the kernel of tradition is present in Paul's thinking just prior to the Temple's destruction.

82. See Appendix B for an explanation of the Gentile categories in Scripture and in Jewish thought (the ger and the goy) as well as the process of becoming and the meaning of a convert in ancient Judaism and modern Judaism.

83. Ro 11:11-12

The expectation that judgment on the Jews was to

bring salvation to the world is a well-founded Jewish tradition, not a tare.

Not so coincidentally, Jewish thought credits the convert (*ger*) with provoking the natural branches to jealousy by their passion for the commandments:

> Gerim are to awaken the Jewish
> people to serve God with fiery
> enthusiasm and meticulous
> observance of the Torah's
> commandments. They cause
> those born Jewish to follow their
> good example and fulfill the
> commandments with an uplifted soul
> and not out of habit or rote. If, God
> forbid, those born Jewish do not take
> inspiration from their example, this
> can cause great accusations to be
> brought against them from Above.
> (ibid p. 163)

The full context of Romans 11 ties together even more Jewish thought concerning the non-Jew who comes to faith in the God of Israel:

> If the first piece of dough is holy, the
> lump is also; and if the root is holy,
> the branches are too. But if some
> of the branches were broken off,
> and you, being a wild olive, were
> grafted in among them and became
> partaker with them of the rich root
> of the olive tree, do not be arrogant
> toward the branches; but if you are
> arrogant, remember that it is not
> you who supports the root, but the
> root supports you. You will say then,
> "Branches were broken off so that I
> might be grafted in." Quite right, they
> were broken off for their unbelief, but
> you stand by your faith. Do not be

conceited, but fear... (v. 16-20)

Paul brings up a point from the Jewish tradition concerning new converts: "Gerim bring arrogance to the Jewish people." (Ben Avraham, 2012, p. 131) In context, this tradition concerns new converts to Judaism. In the First Century, that process was much less formalized than it is today; in fact, it is impossible to say there was a single Judaism of the First Century when Paul lived, but there were Judaisms. There were several sects that were only later homogenized into the generally unified religion known as Orthodox Judaism today. In Paul's First Century mindset, the converts he made among the Gentiles would also have been susceptible to arrogance as were converts to the Jewish people.

The expectation that even righteous Gentiles (converts) could introduce arrogance into their communities and needed to be cautioned is a validated tradition, not a tare.

The First Pentecost?

With no exposure to Jewish tradition, most Christians believe that the first Pentecost is recorded in Acts Chapter Two. In Jewish tradition, however, the first national celebration of Pentecost occurred at Mount Sinai. The Hebrew name of the feast is Shavuot, or the Feast of Weeks. Traditionally, the Torah was given to the Jewish people at Mount Sinai on Shavuot. A summary of that covenant is given by Moses in Deuteronomy:

> Now not with you alone am I making
> this covenant and this oath, but both
> with those who stand here with us
> today in the presence of the LORD
> our God and with those who are not
> with us here today...[84]

84. Deu 29:14-15 In Jewish tradition, the gerim (converts) were those

also standing at Sinai (ibid. p. 193). Additionally, the mixed multitude (*Erev Rav*) that went out of Egypt with the Hebrews played an important role in bringing the nations to the God of Abraham, Isaac, and Jacob. Although the Erev Rav caused problems in the wilderness journey, it is believed in the rabbinic tradition that "The quintessential quality of gerim is that they bring the light of the nations of the world along with them." (ibid., p. 153) In the Book of Revelation, John acknowledges that in the New Jerusalem, the kings of the earth will bring their glory to the Holy City as Jewish tradition says:

> The nations will walk by its light, and
> the kings of the earth will bring their
> glory into it.[85]

What does this have to do with Acts 2? In Acts Two, many proselytes (gerim) had made pilgrimages to Jerusalem to observe the Feast of Shavuot, or Pentecost, which commemorates the giving of the Torah at Sinai. In Jewish expectation, "The Torah was given in 70 languages so that the Erev Rav, who spoke these seventy languages, would in turn purify the seventy original nations of the world." (ibid., p. 58)

When Yeshua's disciples begin proclaiming the gospel in their native tongues in Acts Two, it fulfilled the Jewish expectation that gerim (proselytes, converts) would help to evangelize the nations. Later in the Book of Revelation, John prophesies a return of these righteous gerim to Jerusalem; they are drawn to the Lamp of the Lamb, yet they return with the Light of the Good News from the nations of the earth to the Holy City.

Giving the righteous converts the gospel message at Shavuot (Pentecost) was a "replay" of what occurred in the wilderness at Sinai. The writer of Hebrews 4:2 reminds the reader that the gospel was preached in the wilderness: "For unto us was the

85. Re 21:24

75

gospel preached, as well as unto them: but the word preached did not profit them, not being mixed with faith in them that heard it." The two peoples present at Sinai, the native Hebrew and the ger (convert), did not profit from the gospel given at Sinai because of their lack of faith.

The events in Acts Two at Shavuot were very much a Jewish expectation, yet there had to be a correction of the wilderness failures of both peoples to live that good news according to faith. In Acts Two, the Torah again is proclaimed in the 70 languages of the world to the righteous converts, yet this time it is with the power of the Ruach HaKodesh (Holy Spirit), and it is mixed with superior acts of faithfulness on the part of Yeshua's disciples.

The proclamation of the Torah to the righteous Gentiles at Shavuot is a Jewish tradition grown from truth, not a tare.

A Mark of the Beast: Buying and Selling on Shabbat

Since John wrote so frequently from the Jewish expectation and traditions in the Book of Revelation, what was the Jewish context concerning the mark of the beast? For the non-Jew who is unfamiliar with Jewish law concerning Shabbat (Sabbath), it sounds scary. Oh, no! We won't be able to shop at the grocery store if we don't take the mark? Horrors!

86. For a more thorough study of the mark of the beast, see *Creation Gospel Workbook Four: the Scarlet Harlot and the Crimson Thread* available from www. thecreation gospel.com .

A lack of insight into both the TANAKH (Old Testament) and Jewish tradition concerning the most important number in Revelation, 7, leads to some pretty outlandish conclusions about the mark of the beast. There has been all sorts of speculation concerning what a mark of the beast[86] might be: a computer chip embedded in the hand or forehead, a barcode, a tattoo, a debit card...there's no shortage of ideas.

When one wants to find the significance of a word or number in Scripture, it is important to follow established rules of biblical interpretation called hermeneutics. One rule is First Mention, which means that the first mention of a word or number will establish its significance all the way to the end of Scripture. Other rules are Progressive Mention and Complete Mention, which is locating each mention of that word or number and observing that pattern of significance unfolding. Whatever significance the number 7 has from the beginning to the end of the Bible will be consistent. For example, Shabbat is identified as a day of rest in the week of Creation, and it will be resolved into completion and rest in Revelation.

The Torah instructs humankind to rest on the first 7, Shabbat, and the instruction remains foundational to humankind all the way to Revelation. How does John's traditional Jewish background intersect with the Divine purpose? In Jewish tradition, one does not buy or sell on Shabbat. It is a rabbinic fence that is not explicitly stated in the Torah, yet it is established by ancient Jewish sages and embraced by the Prophets in the TANAKH. *The Concise Code of Jewish Law* explains this rabbinic fence of prohibiting buying and selling on Shabbat: "The purpose of these rabbinic enactments is to keep Shabbat from becoming an ordinary weekday, with people occupying themselves with their usual weekday pursuits." (Appel, p. 97).

The rabbinic fence was not erected in the First Century by scribes and Pharisees, but by the ancient sages, for Nehemiah accepts the fence without question, vowing to keep the gates of Jerusalem closed to the merchants on Shabbat and the special Sabbaths of Israel's feasts. Isaiah 58:13 validates this ancient rabbinic fence, reminding Israel that it dishonors the Sabbath and the One Who gave it to mankind when they pursue their business occupations on that day.

To the Jewish mind, it is the "beast," or the red, hairy Esau character of human beings that continues to occupy itself with normal weekday business on the Sabbath; therefore, no man could buy or sell without the mark of the beast. Esau, also known as Edom, the Red One, is the established Jewish icon of the lower "beastly" human nature that strives against the Holy Spirit. The Jewish prayerbook records a plea, "Deliver us from the Red One!" A clear reference to this prayer of repentance is delivered to the Church of Sardis, which means "Red Ones."

Shabbat is a distinctly spiritual experience, for the physical aspect of life is surrendered to serve the spiritual rest in Messiah. Physical and spiritual become one. What is prepared in six days is surrendered for enjoyment and freedom on the Seventh. The workday burdens are relinquished so that the Divine may be fully embraced. This wholeness of physical and spiritual is the goal of Shabbat, elevating the good work of the weekdays to a state of holiness on Shabbat. A holy Shabbat is not simply a continuation of the workweek, for this gives mankind no rest, nor does it give glory to Adonai as the Creator.

When a human reverences Shabbat and sets it apart to worship the Holy One, he is sealed by the Holy Spirit. When a person dishonors it, he is marked and set apart, for he has identified himself with the beast who was created on the Sixth Day along with the man. Six is the number of both man and beast. The difference? The beast, like Esau, was born first; the man, like Jacob[87], was second born. The apostle Paul says the physical is revealed first, then the spiritual.

However, the spiritual is not first, but the natural; then the spiritual.[88]

87. Yaakov, Jacob's Hebrew name, is from *ekev*, that which follows or comes after.

88. 1 Cor 15:46

The firstborn beast must submit to the rule of the second born man, a being set apart from the animal kingdom because he is made in the image of *Elohim* (Creator God of Genesis 1). One who reverences Shabbat is a man made in the image of Elohim. One

78

who doesn't is conforming to the image of the beast. This has to be rectified, and the Book of Revelation prophesies how it will be accomplished in end times. When the Holy One reveals to the Apostle John this process, He uses the rabbinic fence to illustrate how His Word will be performed.

Is the rabbinic fence of not buying and selling on Shabbat the truth, a tradition, or a tare? It is a tradition grown from the Seed of Truth in the Torah. His Word is Truth. This tradition is not a tare.

Jewish Legal Ruling on Questions of Law

A *psak* is a Jewish legal ruling on matters of practical application of the Torah. The decision of a *posek* is known as a *psak din* or *psak halakha* ("ruling of law") or simply a "psak". In Hebrew, *pasak* is the root implying to "stop" or "cease;" the posek brings the process of legal debate to its final conclusion.

Yeshua issues a *psak* concerning lust. He says looking at a woman in a lustful way is the equivalent of adultery in his heart. Where is the Torah seed of his rendering?

> And you shall not wander after your
> heart and your eyes, which you stray
> after them.[89]

This ruling is upheld by the great Jewish scholar Rambam. This application is a good tradition that grows in good soil from the Seed, not a taredition.

The Commandment to Save Life

There is often confusion about the Jewish emphasis on performing commandments, and non-Jews tend to think that Paul is the first Christian thinker to introduce the idea that there are abuses in the way a person uses the commandments in his or her walk. While the Letter to the Romans can be addressed only in the

89. Nu 15:39

79

briefest way in a booklet, Chapter Ten demonstrates Paul's very Jewish way of understanding the function of the commandments of the Torah as rendered by Moses in Deuteronomy 30.

> For I testify about them that they have a zeal for God, but not in accordance with knowledge. For not knowing about God's righteousness and seeking to establish their own, they did not subject themselves to the righteousness of God. For Christ is the end [goal] of the law for righteousness to everyone who believes. For Moses writes that the man who practices the righteousness which is based on law shall live by that righteousness. But the righteousness based on faith speaks as follows: 'Do not say in your heart, "'Who will ascend into heaven?'" (that is, to bring Christ down), or "'Who will descend into the abyss?'" (that is, to bring Christ up from the dead). But what does it say? ""The word is near you, in your mouth and in your heart""—that is, the word of faith which we are preaching, (Romans 10:2-8)

In this passage, Paul is referring to the most common modern Jewish understanding of the relationship they have to the commandments. He quotes Moses and explains it to the Roman assembly. When certain commandments seem to clash, then the "commandment to preserve life" is cited in Jewish law. For example, although Orthodox Jews do not work or drive on Shabbat, doctors will go to work and ambulance drivers will work and drive. As Yeshua pointed out, the Levites work in the Temple on Shabbat, for those commandments are "weightier."

There is a method of weighing the commandments so that if I need to "break" one in order to keep another, a person can choose to keep the weightier one. In the case of a medical emergency, the commandment to preserve life supersedes the rabbinic law not to drive and the Torah Seed law not to work, for life is at stake. On which passage does Jewish law base this practice and interpretation? The passage from Leviticus 18:5 that Paul quotes above!

> So you shall keep My statutes and
> My judgments, by which a man may
> live if he does them; I am the LORD.

In Judaism, the whole essence of the Torah is contained in this statement. The commandments are not given to kill a precious, holy people, but to give them a place of protection to thrive and live in His Word. The Hebrew prefix *beit* affixed to "by which" can mean "by" or "in." Keeping commandments is not salvation, but sanctification and protection of human life. If we are not living IN them, then we have abused the original intent of the commandments. For this reason, Judaism recognizes the commandment to preserve life, Leviticus 18:5, as superseding all others.

YESHUA AND THE APOSTLES

Yeshua, his disciples, and the apostles all practiced First Century Jewish customs. There are many examples in Scripture, so a few are offered for consideration.

Bar Mitzvah

In Modern Judaism, a boy has his bar mitzvah at the age of thirteen. In the First Century, Yeshua sits in the Temple during the Passover week with the Torah teachers "at about the age of twelve," so it's not a bar mitzvah, right? The *minchag* (local custom) actually varies:

> In the Syrian community, there actually is no set age for a young man to be called to the Sefer Torah for an aliyah. It depends upon the capacity of the individual boy. Many a Syrian lad is called to the Torah around the age of twelve years and six months, in accordance with the halakha... (Angel, 2000, p. 60.)

First Century practice involved much more

doing and being of the commandments; many commandments were fulfilled during the three annual pilgrimages to the Temple in Jerusalem. Modern practice is in comparison more ritualized, for it is based on the remembrance of past practices. A more primitive form of bar mitzvah is practiced by Yeshua. In fact, by bar mitzvah age in the First Century, a boy was supposed to have a command of the Scriptures as well as a command of the Jewish Oral Law. Yeshua's facility with both written and oral law was enough to astound those with whom he sat.

Where is the Seed of this practice? It is in the instructions to teach one's children about the Passover in Exodus 13:8 as well as in Deuteronomy 6:7 and 11:19, which command parents to teach their children the commandments. A bar mitzvah tradition is one way to test both children and their parents for growth from the Seed.

Singing Hallel

Yeshua leads his disciples in the Hallel Psalms (113-118) at Passover. Where is that written in the Torah? It is only in Seed form. It was Jewish tradition that established which Psalms would be sung at the *seder* (service) and when. In fact, over 100 points[90] of theme or practice can be matched from a modern Jewish *haggadah* (order of Passover meal) and the Newer Testament!

Nazirite Vow

90. This chart keying the Newer Testament 100 points of tradition to the modern Jewish haggadah may be found in *Creation Gospel Workbook Six: Standing With Israel.*

Paul agrees to pay for Nazirite vows at Shavuot, the Feast of Weeks. Where is that written in the Torah? It is only in Seed form (and common sense). The seed is found in Numbers 6:

> Now this is the law of the Nazirite
> when the days of his separation
> are fulfilled, he shall bring the
> offering to the doorway of the

84

tent of meeting. He shall present
his offering to the Lord: one male
lamb a year old without defect
for a burnt offering and one ewe-
lamb a year old without defect for
a sin offering and one ram without
defect for a peace offering, and a
basket of unleavened cakes of fine
flour mixed with oil and unleavened
wafers spread with oil, along with
their grain offering and their drink
offering. Then the priest shall present
them before the Lord and shall
offer his sin offering and his burnt
offering. He shall also offer the ram
for a sacrifice of peace offerings to
the Lord, together with the basket
of unleavened cakes; the priest shall
likewise offer its grain offering and
its drink offering. The Nazirite shall
then shave his dedicated head *of
hair* at the doorway of the tent of
meeting, and take the dedicated
hair of his head and put *it* on the fire
which is under the sacrifice of peace
offerings.[91]

Paul, however, is not the one who has taken the
vow, but in order to assure his Jewish brothers that
he is not anti-Torah, he agrees to pay the costs of
the sacrifices on behalf of the ones who did take the
vows:

And when they heard it they *began*
glorifying God; and they said to
him, 'You see, brother, how many
thousands there are among the Jews
of those who have believed, and
they are all zealous for the Law; and
they have been told about you, that
you are teaching all the Jews who
are among the Gentiles to forsake

91. Nu 6:13–18

85

Moses, telling them not to circumcise
their children nor to walk according
to the customs. What, then, is *to be
done?* They will certainly hear that
you have come. Therefore do this
that we tell you. We have four men
who are under a vow; take them
and purify yourself along with them,
and pay their expenses so that they
may shave their heads; and all will
know that there is nothing to the
things which they have been told
about you, but that you yourself also
walk orderly, keeping the Law.'[92]

Agreeing to pay the costs is, to use an American
idiom, "putting your money where your mouth is."
Although Paul's teaching to the Gentiles was not
contrary to the Jerusalem Council's instructions in
Acts 15, rumors were circulating that it was. Paul and
the believing Jewish leadership want to clear up this
rumor, for they have a great reason to celebrate:
thousands of Jews who are zealous for the Torah
have believed!

The actual misunderstanding concerning circumcision and some other topics are addressed in a
booklet entitled *Pharisees: Friends or Foes?*, for the
debate concerning how a new convert should be
initiated into the faith is a very old one within Judaism.
While the believing Jews would have been willing to
debate the details of *how* to teach the Gentiles the
Torah, teaching them to discard it entirely would be
anathema, and the leadership points out to Paul
that the Council had imposed a common starting
place in the Torah for new converts:

But concerning the Gentiles who
have believed, we wrote, having
decided that they should abstain
from meat sacrificed to idols
and from blood and from what is

92. Ac 21:20–24

86

strangled and from fornication."[93]

The Council did not even impose the Big Ten commandments, but some basics to invite table fellowship[94] so the new Gentile believers could learn and gradually shed their pagan habits and beliefs. Paul is on board with this plan:

> Then Paul took the men, and the next day, purifying himself along with them, went into the temple giving notice of the completion of the days of purification, until the sacrifice was offered for each one of them.[95]

Sukkot Water-pouring Ceremony and Month Names

The Prophets and Writings record "Babylonian" names for the months in addition to the Torah's almost exclusive use of numbered months. The Prophets and Writings used non-ordinal names such as Kislev, Ziv, Bul, Tishrei, Etanim, Nisan, Adar, Tevet, etc. Those month-names are not in the Torah, but they are common sense language connections. Babylon has negative connotations, but it was also a place of refuge for the Jews in more than one period of their history. Ancient Semitic languages were, and still are, very similar.

The month of Nissan is closest to the Hebrew word *nis* (#5211), from *nus* #5127, meaning to escape, flee, or save. The First Month of the Hebrew year is the month of Passover when the Israelites escaped from Egypt and were saved. This is also the "green month," Aviv. If the Torah plants a Seed of having an actual month name associated with its theme, the greening of agriculture and firstfruits, then this may explain the later use of names of months in addition to numbers.

The Eighth Month came to be called *Bul*, which means produce, outgrowth; its root is from *yaval*

93. Ac 21:25

94. For a fuller discussion of Peter's vision and table fellowship between Jew and Gentile, see Dr. Robin Gould's booklet: *Peter's Vision: Beacon or Bacon?*

95. Ac 21:26

87

(watercourse, stream, carry along). What happens in the Eighth Month is the outgrowth of the *Yovel* (Jubilee), which is celebrated in the Seventh Month along with the Feast of Trumpets, Day of Atonement, and Tabernacles. The Seventh Month, when the rains begin in Israel, is known by the names *Tishrei* or *Etanim*. Etanim is a perpetually flowing stream, so it makes sense that the Eighth Month of Bul is the continuation of a stream that flowed through the Seventh Month of Etanim/Tishrei.

A beautiful connection is made in the dedication of the First Temple in the Seventh Month, which is called Etanim, in 1 Kings 8 at the Feast of Sukkot. Etanim, "a perpetually flowing stream," holds the secret of Messiah's declaration during the Feast of Tabernacles in the Second Temple:

> Now on the last day, the great day
> of the feast [of Tabernacles/Sukkot],
> Jesus stood and cried out, saying,
> 'If anyone is thirsty, let him come
> to Me and drink. He who believes
> in Me, as the Scripture said, "'From
> his innermost being will flow rivers of
> living water.'"[96]

The feasts, especially the traditional Jewish water-pouring at the feast of Tabernacles, is a perfect tradition that shadowed the work of Messiah, the River of Life bringing restoration of the Spiritual Torah and growing much good fruit.

96. John 7:37-38

7

PLEASE, JUST MAKE IT SIMPLE!

Although it should be simple to distinguish the truth of the Word from a tradition or a tare, sometimes it isn't. It is less difficult to distinguish a tradition from a tare, for tare sentences can't start with "It is written..." In the case of a tradition, it should be accurate to say, "It is written, therefore..." This means that it is my expression of obedience to the written Word since the Word may not define exactly *how* I am to do it. Since the tare disguises itself as a good tradition, however, it will appear as though it is growing from the Seed of the Word, and it will usually present a spiritual component.

No one source can maintain lists of traditions and tareditions, but some examples may help a believer who wants to straighten his or her personal path and to grow in the Word.

The Golden Calf

In Exodus 32 is an excellent example of a taredition. Israel just had an exhilarating, rapturous meeting with the God of their forefathers. It was both terrifying and esoteric, and Moses had climbed the mountain to receive the rest of the message because the Israelites felt that if they heard any more, they would die. As the days go by and Moses is not seen, nor does he return to explain the way forward, many despair and begin to complain. They need a tangible object of worship, not this terrifying *YHVH*[97] and His disappearing messenger Moses.

The High Priest Aaron gives into the demands of those who refuse to overcome their impatience for Moses' return. Aaron takes their gold, melts it, and forms a golden calf. In Exodus 32:4, Aaron declares: "This is your god, O Israel, which brought you up from the Land of Egypt." Aaron then establishes a holiday to honor the substitute god, "A festival for HaShem[98] tomorrow!" (Artscroll TANAKH).

The sin of the golden calf was so egregious that when Moses returns, God strikes Israel with a plague. Moreover, three thousand men were so rebellious that they were unrepentant, and Moses' kinsmen, the Levites, strike them down with swords.

In this Seed story is a template for helping believers distinguish the truth from a tradition or tare. First of all, there is no Seed of truth to the practice of forming a physical object of wood, stone, or metal to worship. The First Commandment is:

> I am the Lord your God, who brought you out of the land of Egypt, out of the house of slavery. You shall have no other gods before Me. You shall not make for yourself an idol, or any likeness of what is in heaven above or on the earth beneath or in the water under the earth. You shall not worship them or serve them...[99]

The truth test stops here, for there is no Seed of truth from which this practice grew. How did the Israelites twist their thinking into believing that is was not only truth, but a valid tradition? A tare RESEMBLES spiritual truth; it spreads its roots into the roots of

97. The Hebrew name of God commonly pronounced as Jehovah in English Bible translations, but many times translated as LORD in the Older Testament.

98. The Jewish substitution for YHVH, which means "The Name." By not writing it or pronouncing it casually, it prevents the Sacred Name from being used casually, being used as a curse word, or for empty oaths, which would bring judgment into the world. When Aaron used the Sacred Name in association with a foreign god, judgment fell by plague and sword.

99. Ex 20:2–5

90

the wheat![100] The Israelites had just been given a Sabbath and specific holy days to celebrate (Exodus 20 & 23); these were truthful, authentic holidays, not holy days mixed with Egyptian spiritual practices or beliefs.

Aaron made it *appear* that the calf was the God that led the Israelites out of Egypt, but it was not! It was only a god. Just because Aaron associated a holy and profound salvation and deliverance with another god could never make the golden calf the God (Elohim) of Abraham, Isaac, and Jacob. Although the Israelites wanted to worship, Aaron could not invent a new holiday for them by fusing it with a foreign god, nor could he force Elohim to like it. A taredition is a violation of a Seed commandment.

If we apply the formula for detecting truth, tradition, or tare, then holidays associated with other gods do not pass the "sniff test" (see Appendix C). It is not truth; therefore, no tradition grown from it can be anything but a taredition even if it closely resembles the truth or incorporates the principles of truth. It erodes the understanding of truth in the mind and heart of the believer, and it is useless even though grown on sincere, good soil. What a waste of good intentions.

The most important considerations in the Prophets', Yeshua's, and the apostles' instructions are that justice, mercy, and faithfulness are the weightier matters of any religious custom. The golden calf does not meet the criteria of faithfulness.

Pretty simple?

Halloween

How about a modern holiday? After all, few believers today would bow down to a golden calf. Granted, the bull on Wall Street has become an icon of faith in the American dollar, and the love of money is the

100. The giving of the Torah at Sinai coincides with the offering of the Firstfruits of the Wheat at the Feast of Weeks, the central feast day of the seven commanded holy feasts.

root of all evil, but perhaps the bull is more iconic of the choice each believer must make in regard to Paul's injunction:

> Therefore consider the members of your earthly body as dead to immorality, impurity, passion, evil desire, and **greed, which amounts to idolatry**. For it is because of these things that the wrath of God will come upon the sons of disobedience…[101]

101. Col 3:5–6

102. Or we might argue a tare, for honoring "saints" was the Church's compromise. The Church permitted blending pagan worship with Christian in order to entice new converts. The convert was invited to add Jesus as one of their gods, and then they were allowed to keep their old gods by simply renaming them as the saints of the Church: "… what used to be done for idols, and is therefore detestable, is done for martyrs, and on that account is acceptable." (MacMullen, 1997, p. 115-116)

The Wall Street bull, however, is not associated with Godly, spiritual behavior; it is strictly secular no matter what amount of passion is invested in money-making. It would never be confused with Jewish or Christian worship by a rational mind. A better example is one that is not a Wall Street bull, yet its commercial value is only exceeded by its value as an erosion to truthful tradition and worship. No bull.

Halloween is a holiday found nowhere in Scripture. Historical research digs up a Christian tradition[102], but no holiday grown in contradiction to the commanded Seed words of Scripture may be added by a believer in Yeshua. A disciple of Yeshua who celebrates Halloween unwittingly transgresses the Seed of the Word:

- Thou shalt not suffer a witch to live. (Ex. 22:18)
- There shall not be found among you anyone who makes his son or his daughter pass through the fire, one who uses divination, one who practices witchcraft, or one who interprets omens, or a sorcerer, or one who casts a spell, or a medium, or a spiritist, or one who calls up the dead. (Deut. 18:10-11)
- You shall be clean before the Lord **and** before Israel. (Numbers 32:22)[103]

Does the God of Israel hate little children and want to cheat them out of an annual sugar-fest and costume party? Isn't it all harmless? There are no idle words in Scripture, and the context assures the reader that the Holy One of Israel does *not* want children to suffer. Our Father never wants a child's life sacrificed, nor has it ever entered His mind.[104]

While the reader may focus on the harsh-sounding imperative against allowing a witch to live within Israel, the Holy God of Israel gives the exact reason why it is so dangerous to let witches and sorcerers practice their craft. The Heavenly Father puts the parent who passes his or her child through the fire in pagan sacrifice into the same sentence with witches and sorcerers. Yikes!

The context gives an additional clue associated with prophecy:

> For whoever does these things is detestable to the Lord; and because of these detestable things the Lord your God will drive them out before you. You shall be blameless before the Lord your God. For those nations, which you shall dispossess, **listen to those who practice witchcraft** and to diviners, but as for you, the Lord your God has not allowed you *to do* so.

"But wait," we say. "I don't actually *believe* in witches and horoscopes and magic numbers! I don't listen to them like a pagan does. There's no harm in it if I don't actually believe in it or worship God like that, is there?" Let's continue reading the context of Deuteronomy 18:12–15 for the truthful and prophetic answer:

> The Lord your God will raise up for you a prophet like me from among

103. In a previous chapter, Paul cites a rabbinic understanding of Numbers 32:22 in I Thessalonians 5:22-23, when he writes: "Abstain from all appearance of evil. And the very God of peace sanctify you wholly; and I pray God your whole spirit and soul and body be preserved blameless unto the coming of our Lord Jesus Christ."

104. Je 19:5

you, from your countrymen, **you shall listen to him**.

The reason for removing the witches and warlocks from the believing community is that it detracts from the words of the prophet like Moses, whom we know is Yeshua the Messiah. There is nothing in Yeshua's words that needs help from a sorcerer! There is nothing in a believer's walk with Yeshua that requires dressing up like a witch or passing out sweets in order to have fun. There is no prophecy of Yeshua that needs assistance from fortunetellers, necromancers, or knocking on wood.

If an adversary wanted to "sell" a golden calf or doctrines of sorcery to the disciples of Yeshua in order to erode the Gospel message, how would he do it? Find the heel or sole of vulnerability and sow the seed near the good Seed. Entwine it around a Christian tradition and make it fun! Sweeten up the way children perceive witches and fortunetellers so that it removes the teaching of the Holy Spirit that such things are dangerous tares in the field of life. Since belief and faith are equivalent, to practice Halloween rituals actually *is* an act of belief, for it is acting upon what one thinks.

If Yeshua's disciples do not mix the Promised Seed of the Word with faithfulness, then it does not profit them, and they will allow the commercial transaction to take place in their hearts until eventually their belief is that it is a harmless bit of fun. They then act on that belief and ignore the Word of truth:

> For unto us was the gospel preached, as well as unto them: but the word preached did not profit them, **not being mixed with faith** in them that heard *it*. For **we which have believed** do enter into rest, as he said, 'As I have sworn in my wrath, if they shall enter into my rest':

94

although the works were finished from the foundation of the world. For he spake in a certain place of the seventh *day* on this wise, 'And God did rest the seventh day from all his works.' And in this *place* again, 'If they shall enter into my rest.' Seeing therefore it remaineth that some must enter therein, and they to whom it was first preached **entered not in because of unbelief.** [105]

The context alludes to the Israelites in the wilderness. The golden calf is celebrated on an added holiday in spite of the clear commandments to the Israelites in the text of Exodus 20 & 23. Moses is taken up out of their sight, and the Israelites soon conceive and believe in a new holiday instead of preparing for and learning about the two kinds of holidays He commanded them: the weekly Sabbath and the seven feasts of Passover, Unleavened Bread, Firstfruits of the Barley, Feast of Weeks, Feast of Trumpets, Day of Atonement, and Tabernacles. If one acts according to the tare, then he has listened to and obeyed that ill-conceived seed word, not the Seed Word.

According to the writer to the Hebrews, the ancient Israelites did not mix the Seed words with faithfulness, so they could not enter the rest of the weekly and annual holy days. They were doomed to fall in the wilderness with their eroded Gospel, for they could not see the important prophecy of Messiah in those holy days. They did not *believe* that Yeshua was central to their God-given Sabbath and holy assemblies. They allowed ungodly Egyptian worship to sow a tare and erode their faithfulness. Although the Israelites in the wilderness were *saved* from bondage, most refused the sanctification of the Word by remaining faithful to it.

While a disciple of Yeshua may not believe in

105. Heb 4:2-6 KJV

sorcery and riding magic brooms, to practice the appearance of it is faithfulness to spiritual power in which he or she claims not to believe! Halloween does not meet Yeshua's criteria of faithfulness. There is no rest in Messiah at a Halloween party, for the believer has "entered in" to the wrong holiday. Ouch!

The Body of Messiah needs to apply Yeshua's tests to every Sabbath and holy day in order to be the lights and lamps of prophecy, for he will return in a cloud and welcome his own to join him with Moses! This is how we "listen" to the prophet like Moses, the one who disappeared into clouds of the Presence of the Father, yet he will reappear at the appointed time. It requires only a small investment of research to locate the Seed and roots of any traditional holy day or Sabbath. Tradition or taredition?

Traditional Holidays

The examples in this chapter are easy-to-identify tares, for in order to do them, a clear commandment *not* to do it is easy to find. When a tradition transgresses a clear commandment, then it is a tare. A tradition, though, may be harder to research. For instance, what about the biblical holidays of Purim in the Book of Esther, Channukah, or the additional fast days listed in the Prophets?

The Eight-day celebration of Channukah starting on Kislev 25 is one example that requires a bit of research, but briefly, the Seed pattern is found in the Torah in the example of the Second Passover for those unable to celebrate at the appointed time, and Leviticus 23 intentionally gives two sets of instructions for the celebration of Sukkot, one for a seven-day celebration, and one with eight days.

Later, two kings of Israel observe double feast celebrations, one a double Passover,[106] and one a double Sukkot. The Prophet Haggai prophesies of

106. 2 Chr 30

an event that will begin in the Ninth Month (Kislev 24), but it is based on something that happened before, when the foundations of the Temple were laid:

> Set now your heart <u>from this day and before, from the twenty-fourth of the ninth month, back to the day when the foundations of the Sanctuary were laid</u>; set your heart: is there any more seed in the silo? Even the grapevine and the fig tree and the pomegranate tree and the olive tree have not borne their fruit. <u>But from this day on</u> I will provide blessing.[107]

When King Solomon celebrated the inauguration of the First Temple Sanctuary, he declared a double Sukkot celebration[108]. The Prophet Haggai plants clues that demonstrate the link between the Seed of the Torah and the [future] celebration of Channukah by posing a question of the priests concerning what is "clean" or "unclean":

> Then Haggai said, 'If one who is unclean from a corpse touches any of these, will the latter become unclean?' And the priests answered, 'It will become unclean.'[109]

If a man had become unclean because of a corpse, then this was the Seed criteria for establishing a second celebration of Passover in Numbers 9:9-10.

Historically, Channukah was a late eight-day celebration of Sukkot because the Sanctuary, the Temple, had not been cleansed from unclean things after the war with the Greeks. This second Sukkot was known as the Feast of Dedication, and the celebration continued every year as a minor holiday. Although the historical celebration was relatively minor (John 10:22), it has taken on more significance in some modern Jewish families who feel that

107. Hag 2:18

108. I Kings 8:65-66

109. Hag 2:13 (NKJV)

they need to provide something to compete with Christmas. It can be challenging to raise children in the midst of these tempting festivals that orginate from tares.

The simple answer is that these holidays must pass the rules concerning the Seed, the tare, and the tradition grown from the Seed. Here are some great questions to ask:

- Is there a Seed Word of the Torah that allows for a commemorative celebration in a day of great deliverance?
- Does the celebration of this day directly violate a "Thou shalt..." or "Thou shalt not..."?
- Does the celebration entwine itself around a Seed of the Word, yet its origin can be definitely placed within a pagan practice?
- Do those who celebrate this day understand that it can never replace the commanded moedim of Adonai?
- Do those who celebrate this day understand that it is not as important or weighty as the commanded moedim?
- Does the celebration draw the glory away from the Holy One of Israel and divert it onto an individual or group of individuals?
- Does the holiday become a point of competition or comparison of one's personal holiness?
- Are there any confirming Scriptures found between the Books of Joshua and Revelation?

You may develop your own questions to get to the root of the celebration or run a soil test.

TEAR THE TARE AND BEAR FRUIT

Tradition, ceremony, ritual, and custom are merely vehicles of rendering the Seed of the Word into the observable world. Most particularly, it binds together the Body of Messiah and creates a sense of "We" as opposed to "I," challenging the doctrines of personal correctness. With the power of the Holy Spirit, there is no room for arrogance in performing the Word.

In the same chapter that Paul writes of *paradosis* to the Corinthians, he assures readers that examining one's self requires a heart-assessment relative to Yeshua's commandments both in obedience to the Word and one's immediate community of faith, for Paul says that failure to give Light to the Body at the feasts makes the individual sick. It is a rocky road to grow in the Word when its observance and personal motivations are sickly.

Yeshua left easy instructions for growing in the Word. First, the action demonstrates faithfulness to the written Word; it is an obedient action or inaction based on a clear "It is written…" or "You shall not…" If a diligent search of the Word does not yield the Seed, then it is likely a tare to tear down, especially if it is designed to skirt the actual commandment. Second, the individual should know the difference between the Seed and his practice that renders that

Seed into the physical world; distinguishing the Seed from the custom should remind the observer that the practice is not as important as the Word itself.

The criteria of justice and mercy demonstrate the essence of the Torah, which is to love one's neighbor. [110] Justice, or tzedekah, is not just fairness, but the catalyst that lifts the countenance of all believers toward the Light of the Lamp, Yeshua. The Torah is a Light, and the commandment is a Lamp, so any observance of a commandment should *give* the Light of the Creator to others.

Do others feel the favor of Adonai when I keep a commandment? If my observance is a way for the Holy Spirit to convict someone of transgressions, then that is out of my hands, but if I am diligent to convey the absolute joy of obedience, then even in conviction, the Light of truth can turn to favor. It is egregious to clobber a fellow-servant of Yeshua with commandments.

The point of giving the Torah to Israel was so that the nations would recognize the brilliant wisdom and understanding of Israel's God. Justice is to weigh and do what ethically is right with its scales so that the physically or spiritually poor or weak are brought into balance with those who have more. Those same scales will identify when tradition begins to weigh more heavily than truth. This critical definition of tzedekah as justice leads back to the foundational text in Psalm 97:11:

> **Light is sown like seed** for the
> righteous and gladness for the
> upright in heart.

The "righteous" in the text is the *tzaddik*, a noun formed from the same root as tzedekah, or justice. The righteous person is the one who does what is right: he or she gives the Light of the Word to others by loving them with the commandments. According

110. Lev 19:18

to the text, when the *tzaddik*[111] sows Light to grow light, the result is gladness. The caveat is that such Light will resonate with the "upright in heart," not necessarily those who love darkness.

Because of the mercy inherent in the commandments, people with upright hearts from all the nations experience Adonai's lovingkindness, and they understand Yeshua's reassurance that they are not burdensome[112], but an easy yoke. For this reason, observing commandments or traditions in order to draw attention to the individual is a transgression of the essence and purpose of God's teachings and instructions.

Customs, traditions, and practices are not what give life to the observer; it is the Seed of the Word that stimulates growth:

> You are to perform My judgments
> and keep My statutes, to live in
> accord with them; I am the Lord your
> God. So you shall keep My statutes
> and My judgments, **by** which a man
> may live if he does them; I am the
> Lord.[113]

A process of sanctification and growth from the Seed should occur once a person comes to faith in the God of Abraham, Isaac, and Jacob, the Holy One of Israel. Yeshua and his apostles urge this growth in the life of the believer, emphasizing the weight of "It is written....," not "I feel..." The custom or tradition aids the disciple of Yeshua in living out that life-giving Word in a practical way. It offers a sense of community and clarity in a life of progressive sanctification.

Keeping commandments is for growth, not salvation, and obedience to the commandments is Yeshua's righteousness, not the individual's. It is Messiah's righteous clothes of obedience that one acquires

111. In the Newer Testament, the tzaddik is usually translated as a "saint."

112. Mt 11:29-30

113. Lev 18:4–5

and wears to clothe nakedness.[114] Believers live *in* Yeshua's clothes of the commandments, but they are not the manufacturers of them. We acquire them with faithfulness to live as he did. Revelation 3:18 urges:

> I advise you **to buy from Me** gold refined by fire so that you may become rich, and white garments so that you may clothe yourself, and that the shame of your nakedness will not be revealed..."

Although John writes in Greek, the Hebrew word *liknot*, to buy, has a dual meaning of "to acquire," not only to pay money. In Jewish tradition, the commandments become spiritual clothes for the afterlife, and without them, one experiences shame at judgment. Transgressions are stains that must be "bleached" from those clothes through confession and repentance.

Adonai assures His people that though their sins are like scarlet that He will make them as white as snow; Adonai will accept their repentance and forgive their transgressions. Jewish Law considers snow a primary cleansing agent (*hamlaben*) along with water. (Appel, p. 153) If a tradition or custom helps a disciple of Yeshua to stay clothed in Yeshua's commandments and raises awareness of transgressions, then by all means, remain clothed! This honors the blood shed by Messiah and prevents the shame of nakedness.

In some cases, the Jewish law was put in place to preserve the life of the disciple. Because some commandments carry the death penalty or very severe punishments, the goal was to preserve life by adding a fence of custom to make it harder for the individual to violate a commandment that requires loss of life. The commandments are designed to give
114. Rev 3:17 life, not death, and the heart of the Jewish sages was

to preserve life with the fences, not for anyone to mistake the fences for the actual commandments.

On the other hand, there may be so many fences in place that the person begins to "die" in them or to mistake the custom for the commandment itself.[115] The fences may become so onerous that while it becomes harder to violate a death-penalty commandment, it also becomes harder to prosper in the life of the commandment. The Jewish way of reading Leviticus 18:4-5 is that if the goal of the Torah is to give the faithful a way of living *in* it, then by its nature, it should not take away life.

From this reasoning, Jewish discussions and commentaries often reference a common understanding that "the commandment to preserve life supersedes all other commandments." (Appel, p. 88) For instance, if Orthodox Jews do not drive automobiles on Shabbat so that they will not "kindle a fire," yet someone has a medical emergency, the person will be taken to the hospital without delay or an ambulance called. Why?

Yeshua applied this principle in his example of David eating the showbread when he was a fugitive from King Saul. While he was not permitted by the Torah to eat the holy things, his hunger and lack of resources demanded that he be given life in the Tabernacle; therefore, David was given the showbread. This did not negate the Torah's intention of keeping the holy bread only for the priests, but that commandment did not demand David's life in order to preserve it. This is *kal v'chomer*, the light and heavy test.

Likewise, Modern Judaism emphasizes that it is better to violate a rabbinic prohibition than an actual commandment of the Torah. Even then, the preservation of life is the Spirit of the Torah, and if it is necessary to violate a commandment in order to live in the Word, then it is permitted.

115. Jewish law clearly makes a distinction between Torah law and rabbinic law, and it is very definite in urging Jews to break a rabbinic law rather than a Torah law if one must be broken. (Appel, 2016, 99-100) This does not prevent individuals, however, from mistaking one for the other because of lack of interest in distinguishing the difference. Similarly, it does not prevent individuals from emphasizing the rabbinic law in order to draw attention to one's piety.

Non-Jews have a lot of freedom to live in the Word, growing fruits of the Spirit in simple practices or those defined in Judaism. It is not necessary to become Jewish and take on *all* tradition, for Paul was as clear about this as he was about passing on Jewish tradition. If it meets the test of the Seed, and it brings joy and life, then feel free to remember and keep the Word through some traditions. Whether Jew or Gentile, scorning, belittling, or mocking those who keep more or less tradition, however, is not a way to make the way straight for Messiah's return.

Yeshua did not tear down tradition, but taredition. Yeshua did not uproot and replant the Seeds of truth grown in good soil, but in rocky, shallow soil. The words of Scripture are a Tree of Life to those who take hold of them, and when the Seeds of the Word are grown on good soil, they produce healthy trees with good fruit.

Whether obeying the instructions of the Seed itself or finding an expression of the Seed through tradition, custom, or practice, the outcome will be the same. We will be loving, living, giving lamps of Light to the world:

> By this we know that we love the
> children of God, when we love
> God, and keep his commandments.
> For this is the love of God, that we
> keep his commandments: and his
> commandments are not grievous.
> [116]

116. 1 John 5:2-3

FLOW CHART LEGEND: TRUTH, TRADITION, OR TARE?

- Select a tradition. Is it grown from Seed of Torah? Does the tradition lead the individual into observing the actual Word (faithfulness), the Word of Truth?
- If the tradition is a clear violation of the Seed of the Word, then it is a taredition. Stop, uproot it, and discard it. If it helps, list the verses that prohibit the tradition.
- If there is no clear commandment against the practice, but you can't locate the actual Seed Word, then research to find out if there is a source that might reference the Seed, such as the Jewish traditions of Rosh HaShanah in this booklet. It's possible that you haven't yet identified the Seed through continued study. Put your question on the shelf until you have time to study more.
- If the tradition is rooted in the Seed of the Word, list the Seed verses.
- Heart check. Does the tradition purposely draw attention and admiration to the individual practicing it instead of the Father? If so, commence heart repair through repentance, uproot it, and replant the Seed

in better soil: a clean, servant's heart of flesh.

- Heart check. Does the tradition replace the Seed of the Word or give the tradition more importance ("weight") than the Seed itself? If so, commence heart repair through repentance, uproot it, and replant the Seed in better soil: a clean, servant's heart of flesh.
- Heart check. Does the tradition uphold the heart of the Torah, mercy, justice, and faithfulness? If not, commence heart repair through repentance, uproot it, and replant the Seed in better soil: a clean, servant's heart of flesh.
- If the tradition passes the Heart Check, then keep growing in the Word!

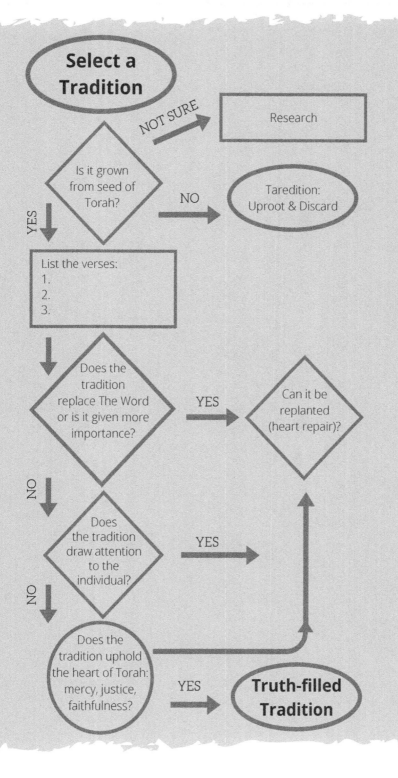

QUESTIONS AND CHALLENGES FOR REVIEW

1. What three things are the "heart" of any commandment? Define them.

2. Explain how a tradition can grow from the Seed of the Word.

3. Explain how a tare grows.

4. Explain what happens when the good Seed grows on rocky or shallow soil.

5. Summarize Yeshua's lesson in the parable of the tax collector and the Pharisee.

6. Give some examples of how Yeshua or Paul practiced or encouraged keeping Jewish traditions.

7. List four or five parallels between the Jewish traditions of Rosh HaShanah and the message to the Church of Sardis.

8. Do you think that it ever occurred to the Jerusalem Council in Acts 15 that non-Jews would come to worship apart from their Jewish brothers and sisters? Why or why not?

9. Explain what role tradition has to the following:

> "You are to perform My judgments and keep My statutes, to live in accord with them; I am the Lord your God. So you shall keep My statutes and My judgments, **by** which a man may live if he does them; I am the Lord."

10. Pick one or more holidays that you celebrate, and research the origin. Next, apply Yeshua's tests of validity and good soil. What is your conclusion? Seed Word or taredition? Good soil or bad?

APPENDIX A

The Seven Spirits of Adonai

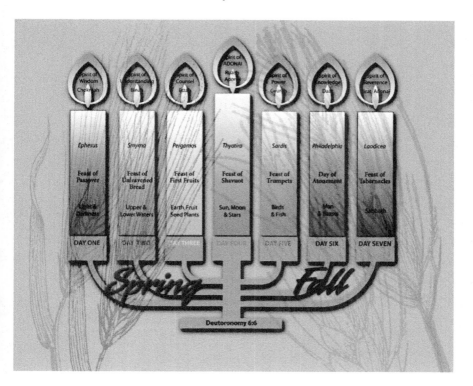

APPENDIX B

Converts Then and Now

The First Century represents a time of transition in which many life events or customs that were informal practices or commonly-held beliefs until the destruction of the Temple became codified into Jewish Law; this occurred in order to preserve Jewish identity post-Temple destruction (see *Introduction to the Jewish Sources* by S. Creeger for a brief history). For instance, the more formalized Passover seder practiced today was a time-intensive and less formal process when the Temple stood. The actual pilgrimage trip would have been a major undertaking, and the lamb sacrifice and ritual meal were much more "hands-on," for the family was **doing** the actual Passover as opposed to merely **remembering** the Passover.

Like the example of the Passover seder, the very formal conversion process experienced today by those who convert to Judaism is in contrast to ancient times, such as when a *goy* (Gentile, a person from any other nation than Israel) or *nakar* (stranger) such as Rahab or Ruth converted by simply making a declaration of attachment to the Israelite people and their God and by living according to the covenant commandments given at Sinai. For the male, circumcision was required, and by the First Century, both male and female would immerse in a *mikveh* (immersion pool) with the expectation that upon emerging from the water, the person would be a brand new person, a Jew.

Yeshua mentions this immersion to Nicodemus, a respected member of the Jewish Sanhedrin, not a convert to Judaism. His implication is that even the native born Israelite needs to be spiritually renewed to keep the Torah given at Sinai, just as the Gentile convert needs the mikveh to represent his new birth as a Jew committed to the covenant. The circumcision of the flesh eventually must be matched by circumcision of the Spirit. While the Gentile convert would accept circumcision as a LAST sign of the covenant, being circumcised of the heart FIRST, the circumcised Jew experienced a FIRST circumcision on the Eighth

Day, yet a LAST circumcision of the heart, something consciously desired and embraced as he or she grew up in the faith.

A convert in Modern Judaism is known as a *ger*. A ger is someone who is not a native-born Israelite, but who desires to draw close and accept the covenant upon themselves. Modern Judaism considers such a person a proselyte, yet a full-fledged Jew once the conversion process is complete. The Torah describes the ger as one who desires to keep the Passover, and therefore consents to circumcision to take on the whole Torah and become part of Israel:

> And when a **stranger** shall sojourn
> with thee, and will keep the passover
> to the LORD, let all his males be
> circumcised, and then let him come
> near and keep it; and he shall be
> as one that is born in the land: for
> no uncircumcised person shall eat
> thereof. One law shall be to him that
> is homeborn, and unto the **stranger**
> that sojourneth among you. (Exodus
> 12:48-49)

First Century rabbinic disagreements concerning exactly what was required of a ger were probably responsible for much of the controversy surrounding the Gentile converts made by the Jewish apostles in the First Century, a topic addressed in a BEKY Book entitled *Pharisees: Friends or Foes?* The disagreements would have likely involved Exodus 12:48-49, yet more Seed texts come into play with the issue of circumcision for males.

APPENDIX C

The Sniff Test

And there shall come forth a rod out of the stem of Jesse, and a Branch shall grow out of his roots: and the spirit of the LORD shall rest upon him, the spirit of wisdom and understanding, the spirit of counsel and might, the spirit of knowledge and of the fear of the LORD; and shall make him of **quick understanding** in the fear of the LORD: and he shall not judge after the sight of his eyes, neither reprove after the hearing of his ears: But with righteousness shall he judge the poor, and reprove with equity for the meek of the earth: and he shall smite the earth with the rod of his mouth, and with the breath of his lips shall he slay the wicked.

When the text says that the Branch will be of quick understanding, in Hebrew it implies a sense of smell, *reyach*, or an odor, *ruach*, a root related to *ruach*, or spirit; in fact, traditional Jewish teaching says that the Messiah will judge cases by his sense of SMELL. He will be able to sniff out what cannot be seen and heard plainly, but he will judge with a gift of intuition for truth. Additional insight into the text says that not judging after the sight of the eyes is not judging by mere appearance, and not reproving after the hearing of the ears is not judging based on rumors. Instead, this judge waits for the facts and weighs them.

APPENDIX D

Summary of the Seven Feasts (Moedim) of Adonai

Passover	Unleavened Bread	Firstfruits of the Barley	Weeks
• aka: Pesach commemorates the Exodus from Egypt	• aka: Chag MaMatzot • removal of leaven (sin) from home through diligent search	• aka: Yom HaBikkurim • elevation of the firstfruits of the barley each year, symbolic of resurrection	• aka: Firstfruits of the Wheat or Shavuot • Celebrates giving of the Torah

Trumpets	Atonement	Tabernacles
• aka:Yom Teruah, Rosh HaShanah • Day of Remembrance and a judgment day as well as a day of repentance	• aka: Yom HaKippurim, The Day [of judgment] • fast day and atonement by sacrificing two goats to cover and remove sin	• aka: Sukkot, Booths, Feast of the Nations • Firstfruits of all produce, livestock and rejoicing in the Torah

REFERENCES

Alt-Miller, Y. (2011). *Angels at the table: a practical guide to celebrating Shabbat.* New York: Continuum International Publishing Group.

Angel, M. (2000). *Exploring Sephardic customs and traditions.* Brooklyn, NY: Ktav Publishing House.

Appel, G. (2016). *Concise code of Jewish law: A guide to the observance of Shabbat.* D. Goldstein, Ed. New York: Maggid.

Ben Avraham, D. (2012). *Bnei Avraham Ahuvecha: gerim in Chassidic thought.* Charleston: Createspace.

Ganor, O. (2016). *The Transformation.* Digital newsletter. Jerusalem: Ulpan-Or. Email dated 9/29/16 2:04pm.

MacMullen, R. (1997). *Christianity and paganism in the fourth to eighth centuries.* Connecticut: Yale University Press.

Yerushalmi, M. (2007). *From Baghdad to Jerusalem.* E. Yerushalmi & D. Yerushalmi, Trans. Tel Aviv: Kotarot Publishing. Originally published as *The Journey of Abu-Moch.*

ABOUT THE AUTHOR

Dr. Hollisa Alewine has her B.S. and M.Ed. from Texas A&M and a Doctorate from Oxford Graduate School; she is the author of *Standing with Israel: A House of Prayer for All Nations*, The Creation Gospel Bible study series, and a programmer on Hebraic Roots Network. Dr. Alewine is a student and teacher of the Word of God.

Made in the USA
Coppell, TX
05 December 2021

67171864R00069